CRAWLING IN THE DARK:

SEARCHING FOR THE LIGHT

CRAWLING IN THE DARK:

SEARCHING FOR THE LIGHT

by Patrick Sprankle

Cover Artwork provided by Tim Murphy

ISBN: 978-155605-390-0

Library of Congress Control Number: 2008938365

WYNDHAM HALL PRESS
Lima, Ohio 45806
www.wyndhamhallpress.com

Printed in The United States of America

TABLE OF CONTENTS

ACKNOWLEDGEMENTS

One of my favorite holidays is Thanksgiving. Not only do we create and celebrate an awesome meal, but we gather with family and friends, many times in the cold and dreariness of a new winter. As I wrote this book, I was once again very thankful for the family and friends who, because of God's presence in them, gathered around me and supported the work (even when it seemed cold and dreary!)

I am first deeply thankful for my wife, Lee Ann, always my best friend and companion in faith and sacrament. I love you! I am also so thankful to my son Matt and daughters, Meghan and Lauren. You show me the love of God everyday and make me want to be a better father and human. Mom and Dad, you have shown me the gift of parenting (and grand parenting) by your loving example and were the first to introduce me to Jesus. Thank you so much for your constant commitment, care and faith. Pat and Joan, you are incredible parents-in-law and grandparents, daily expressing your love to us. And my brothers and sisters (outlaw and in-law), I am so blessed to be a part of this family.

And to my other family, those brothers and sisters I have come to know and love through the youth ministry community. Thanks to Bob McCarty (friend, mentor and project supervisor) and Maggie McCarty, Mark and Carol Pacione, Ted Miles, Helene Murtha, my spiritual director, Fr. Joe Muth, and all who walk with Jesus in ministering to young people. Steve Angrisano, thanks for your words of wisdom in the forward of this book and for your constant witness of faith.

Special gratitude to Msgr. Joseph Luca (Pastor) and to the staff and parishioners of St. Louis Church, and especially the Youth Ministry & Religious Education Offices (DREYM Team!) for your service to the church and making my time at the church a great blessing.

A big thanks to all of those young people with whom I have worked and walked over the years, but especially for those helped make this book happen. Lauren and Adam, I chose well the first two young adults to preview this book. Your words of support, your wisdom and your example of faith are a blessing to me. Tim Murphy, Stephen Fry and Annie Marcotte, your artwork speaks so eloquently what God has done in your life. Caitlin, Robert, Andrea, Liz, Jane and all of those young people who have shared their faith stories (either written or spoken), thanks for the privilege to listen.

And finally, thanks also to two powerhouses: the Msgr. Clare O'Dwyer Retreat House, which has served young people in the Archdiocese of Baltimore for over 45 years and where I spent time as adjunct director (and writing this book!) and the Franciscan Friars Conventual in Ellicott City, Maryland, for allowing me to invade their beautiful library on several occasions.

FOREWORD

I have known Pat Sprankle for a long time and what a blessing it has been in my life. Pat is, simply put, one of the best youth ministers in the country today. As long as I've known him, I have marveled at how he just seems to be able to see right through to a person's heart. You know what I'm talking about...

I have always had the feeling that, whenever Pat asks, "How are you doing?", a one word answer is just not gonna cut it... Not because he requires anything more, but because he can usually see that there IS more. Pat is one of those people that, if you are having a really terrible day, but still manage to spit out an 'academy award' quality, "oh, I'm fine" He is very likely to say, "Really?"

That's why I knew, when Pat sent me this book, it was going to be special. I can't think of anyone who could do a better job of wrestling with tough questions like this with teenagers. He has been there, in the lives of so MANY teenagers at tough times, more often than most.

I love how this book encourages all of us, particularly young people, to be unafraid of our doubts. Pat helps us to realize that part of growing up is asking questions about things we have been told, 'searching in the dark' so to speak. I wish someone could have told me this when I was in High School! I was so afraid that my questions were somehow not ok. This book would have meant so much to me. As a parent, I really appreciate the concrete insight for parents. It is certainly good to know that if part of developing an adult faith is asking questions, I should probably not "freak out" when my kids express their own doubts! It is my love and patience that I can give them that will prove most valuable.

Also, I think the insight on how technology affects our relationships is one of the most insightful things I've read in a long time. Constant contact by email and text message is not the same thing as intimacy. Ironically, we become more "separate" from others, while thinking we are closer! In this way, we can lose our perspective. This has a real and negative effect on all our relationships including (maybe even especially) our relationship with God.

I know you will enjoy this book as much as I did and it is my prayer that what Pat has done here will encourage all of us, in moments of spiritual darkness, to know that we are not alone. I pray for all of us, with flashlight in hand, to be unafraid to seek out the gentle loving God that holds us in His hands is waiting patiently for us.

Steve Angrisano,
Musician, Speaker

I. CRAWLING IN THE DARK

Crawling around in the dark is not fun. I remember having to crawl way back into a crawl space in my Nanna's basement each holiday to get all of the decorations she needed for that particular season. I would bump my head, cursing quietly each time I bruised not only my scalp but my knees as I knelt then crawled, knelt then  *crawled. Finally, the experience was over for another couple of months as I crawled towards the light and my grandmother's thankful smile.*

Thinking back on this experience still brings to mind certain feelings. The goal of helping my grandmother was a worthwhile one, but I'll never forget the other feelings and thoughts that accompanied the experience of crawling in the darkness, feelings of **fear** (large spiders and deep darkness!) **panic** (getting lost), and sometimes even **anger** (lack of light switches and evil steel beams!) I have often remembered this experience since then, when I encountered these same feelings in different circumstances, particularly those dealing with spirituality.

Those of us who encounter the darkness of doubt concerning our faith and beliefs in God, religion and purpose in life may sometimes feel fear, panic and anger. The sheer intensity of the questionings, sometimes coupled with the triggers that may cause doubt, can be overwhelming.

What is doubt then? It might be crawling through a "feeling of not knowing what to believe or what to do, or the condition of being uncertain" (1) or the darkness that accompanies "thinking something unlikely or not trusting somebody or something." (2)

Doubts can be about faith in God, individuals, institutions (religions, politics, etc), values and morality, ways of living, and more. Doubts can make one grow and get stronger or can stunt growth and cause unhealthy thoughts and actions. Doubts can be brought on by inner or outside influences, by choices that we make or circumstances beyond our control. We can doubt about something specific ("Why, God, did you let this person die?") or about something general ("Not sure I believe in the whole 'God' thing.") Feelings while doubting, depending on the intensity of the uncertainty and who or what is the object of the doubt, can run the gamut from fear to panic to anger to loneliness to silence!

Called "Crawling In The Dark:" Searching for the Light," this book will try to shed some light on the crawl spaces of our souls, revealing that doubts are as much a part of spirituality as faith. We will explore four reasons why spiritual people, specifically young people, have doubts. Young people doubt because:

(1.) it is natural for us all as humans and for you as young people;

(2.) we encounter inner and outside influences or voices;

(3.) we have personally witnessed suffering or evil;

(4.) we have turned away from truth, goodness and God and are looking in the wrong places for answers and happiness.

We will also discuss practical strategies and provide directions concerning what can be done when questions and faith struggles occur. In short, this book is written about what to do when you are crawling in the darkness of your soul, or making your way through the uncertainties of faith. It is for people who are not sure what to believe or who to trust.

Read the lyrics of a deeply spiritual song by Hoobastank, called Crawling in the Dark. The words make the above definition of doubt come alive. As we read, we see one man's search for understanding and direction. It is between the searcher and God whether this crawling will have a positive or negative outcome:

"I will dedicate and sacrifice my everything for just a second's worth of how my story's ending and I wish I could know the directions that I take and all the choices that I make won't end up all for nothing. Show me what it's for, make me understand it. I've been crawling in the dark looking for the answer. Help me carry on. Assure me it's okay to use my heart and not my eyes to navigate the darkness…Because I'm looking and I just can't see what's in front of me." (3)

In this song, the lead singer laments his wandering in the darkness and will give anything and everything to receive help, direction and answers…in a sense, light! He implies that our eyes can sometimes deceive us…In a world where 'seeing is believing' and where data and physical evidence defines what is important and 'true,' the singer knows that it is what lies in our hearts that matters.

There are several things I've noticed from my interactions with the darkness, whether they be in my grandmother's crawlspace or in times of doubting. First, it is very natural to want to protect myself by putting feelers out, i.e., hands or feet or even sticks that scout out trouble ahead of me. Secondly, it is very ordinary to be on the lookout for the light, hoping against hope that a hanging bulb or switch is right around the next corner. And finally, the darkness tends to be less dark and overwhelming if there is someone else with you. Yes, these three tricks for dealing with the dark (using feelers to protect and find the way, looking for the light, and finding someone with whom to share the darkness) are handy for those of us who struggle with the dark and want to emerge victorious!

The image of a person with hands or feet extended, attempting to maneuver through a darkened room, does serve as an appropriate analogy for times of doubt and questioning. Using our 'feelers,' we must not only strike out blindly and carefully when uncertain, but we must trust in past experiences where our limbs have done the job for us and our memories remind us of steel beams. Using familiar thought processes to discover the way, courageously asking the right questions (or asking any questions at all), being open to new directions, and intuitively knowing when to duck or change course, are all important when finding our way through the dark times. What does your spirituality look like during this time and what feelers do you have out to get to the light?

Because we sometimes panic in the dark, we forget to keep our mind, heart and spirit looking ahead to the 'light at the end of the tunnel.' Although it may seem like the darkness is ever pervasive and the night ever lasting, there is hope and light. The story of the Israelites wandering in the desert illustrates how people sometimes forget the Promised Land.

"The Israelites managed to waste forty years lost in a relatively small desert, an area smaller than the state of New Jersey. They knew the sun set in the west, they knew the North Star, they were not geographic idiots. And, as mentioned, God guided them. But they grew weary and lost their vision and hope for the Promised Land. And for an extended period, they settled....They gave up not only on the destination, but even on the journey. (4)

Before you settle in the darkness, lose your vision or hope and despair of questioning, think back to the last insight you received when you were having a problem at school or in a relationship. Call me an optimist, but I believe there is good around every corner. Maybe a pro mised land of sorts; it is a skill to be able to glimpse that good, that light, much like the skill of practicing and performing in sports or drama. Sometimes, it is the choice of wandering and crawling (which take up a lot of energy) or actively and persistently seeking the light.

Finally, having friends or companions makes the darkness seem easier to swallow. If there are others who have gone before us to survive and thrive in the darkness, don't these pioneers make us more confident that we too will make it through? If there is someone walking right next to us as we grope along, doesn't the room seem a little less scary? In this book, you can listen to others who have walked the darkness, young people much like yourself who have written essays of reflection or offered artwork on their own times of doubt and despair, and some maybe surprising famous people who have lost the way and offer advice. They are highlighted throughout the book to give you insight, support and maybe even a sense that you are not in it alone.

John of the Cross, one of the saints of the Catholic Church, has some pretty awesome things to say about his own dark times. In his Ascent of Mount Carmel, he says:

"I believe you are learning how faith is a dark night of the soul and how the soul as well must be dark-or in darkness as to its own light-that it may allow itself to be guided by faith to this high goal of union...Like the blind, people must lean on dark faith, accept it for their guide and light, and rest on nothing of what they understand, taste, feel, or imagine. All these perceptions are a darkness that will lead them astray. Faith lies beyond all this understanding, taste, feeling, and imagining." (5)

The 'dark night of the soul?' Pretty scary stuff, huh? But, crawling in the dark is also sometimes scary. Trust me! There is much to be said for being open to what is out there, and, more specifically, to the place that your spirituality is right now. There is also much to be said for keeping your ears open to the wisdom and relevant experience of saints like John of the Cross, or, more recently, Mother Teresa, who speak words of comfort and relevance to our own lives because of their own struggles. Mother Teresa's own self-proclaimed period of darkness, or Le Tenche, lasted from 1949-1997, quite a long time to be crawling in the dark! And yet, her knees weren't rug burned from crawling but from kneeling and praying…for 48 years!

I am longing with painful longing to be all for God, to be holy in such a way that Jesus can live His life to the full in me. The more I want Him, the less I am wanted. I want to love Him as He has not been loved, and yet there is that separation, that terrible emptiness, that feeling of absence of God. I did not know that love could make one suffer so much. That was suffering of loss, this is of longing, of pain human but guided by the divine. "I have come to love the darkness, for I believe now that it is a part, a very very small part of Jesus' darkness and pain on earth." (6)

Maybe your darkness is like Mother Teresa's and you are having questions about your life, about God, about your place in the world. Maybe you experienced death or divorce or abuse or violence or natural disaster and are wondering why. Maybe you met someone at school or in your neighborhood or on the internet or even in church who introduced you to totally different questions or doubts, or to dabbling with a completely different spirituality. Maybe you made a choice to do something that you had previously thought you would never do, that you had thought was wrong, something that you feel guilty about and, over time, believe that God has abandoned you. Maybe you have a friend for whatever reason is struggling with faith right now and you want to know what to do or say. As a youth minister, I have come to respect this sometimes painful, sometimes confusing, sometimes frustrating, but always real time in a young person's life. I have had the opportunity, the privilege to talk and more importantly to listen to individuals and groups about the above scenarios.

Jim, a star athlete at a local public school, was devastated after the tragedy of 911. He told his mom that he could not make sense of it, nor could he believe in a God who would allow it to happen. Even in his unbelief, Jim decided that he would pray and lit up the outside patio of his house with 9-11 individual candles. Jessica was then a high school senior who came into my office at the church in tears. She said that she never felt farther away from God then now.

As I listened, she shared a very difficult situation about getting pregnant and feeling no option but to have an abortion. Although it had happened over 7 months before, Jessica's feelings of guilt and loneliness made her think that God did not want to have anything to do with her anymore. Bill sits in church, feeling bored and unconnected to what is happening before him. He thinks that he has moved beyond the childish and irrelevant 'church of his parents.' He has more complaints than compliments for his priests, his religious education classes and the faith in which he grew up. Now he feels he has grown out of it. Caitlin met another young woman recently on a myspace page, someone who seems really friendly and interested in her. They have been chatting about witchcraft and WICCA, and her friend is really trying to get Caitlin to experiment with this 'earthy' religion.

Wherever *you* are in your faith, is there someone who has respected or appreciated your journey? A little while ago, I made a mistake in a high school class I was teaching. I asked them to write on an index card any questions they might have about their faith, about being Catholic, about morality. A good one third of them wrote things like 'What should I write?" and "I don't have any questions." One even made up a philosophical 'stumper' question (akin to the 'which came first: The chicken or egg' legend). I realized that not everyone may be at a point where they are wondering (or wandering in the dark), but everyone will be at that point at sometime in their life. Now, I ask people to write either a statement of faith (these are pretty powerful) or a question they might have so we can have an open and honest dialogue. My desire is not to play "Answer Man," although sometimes a clear answer about what we believe is necessary. My real desire is to just be there with young people, to sit with them and listen to the struggles and the strengths of the soul.

My grandmother, now deceased but ever in my thoughts, used to desire only a few things of me. One was my crawling around in the dark, but the other was to just come and sit with her for awhile....Nothing more, nothing less. Just sit and rest awhile, have a soda, put up our feet and enjoy the time together. Hopefully, you can do the same with these reflections. And although my own journey of faith and beliefs will sometimes be very evident, I will try not to convince you of anything... Your questions and your faith life are too important for that.

I do encourage you, though, to take some time (soda in hand and feet up optional) and go a little deeper. Wherever you are in your beliefs about God, religion, suffering, sin, mercy, justice or whatever, do a little meditating for yourself. Our lives are literally spent in darkness half the time...Depending on where you live, your nighttime can be around 12 hours long. So, it's what you do with the dark that is important. God created light out of darkness and chaos. Get used to the fact that darkness is a part of spirituality. Only then can we appreciate the light of day.

So, I respectfully and sincerely invite you to take some time for your spirit by reading this book. Look for that one insight that might give you a deeper understanding of who you are as a spiritual person, a light for the darkness if you will. Listen to other's struggles and stories of faith and the crawling may not seem as hard. In fact, as you read this book, let's not crawl anywhere together. Let's walk carefully and gently, respecting each other on this journey of spirituality.

QUESTIONS FOR REFLECTION:

1. What (or who) originally drew you to this book?

2. How would you describe your own journey of the spirit?

3. What might be one personal goal or desire that you have?

II. NATURAL THIRST

It was August and my family had decided to take our annual end-of- summer trip, this time to Maine. We traveled (the long way, it seems) to Bar Harbor and Acadia National Park. That night, during a late dinner, we asked the server for the lowdown on great hiking spots. She gave us a few and then her eyes lit up and she said, "You have to do The Precipice while you're here, though! This is the only place on the East Coast where the ocean meets such majestic mountains!" The next day, after a heavy thundershower, we explored Thunder Hole (a hole between two large rocks which receives waves from the ocean with a loud roar) and Cadillac Mountain, and soon found The Precipice. After reading the sign at the bottom (.8 miles to the top, part of which was iron ladder and rungs to guide you...), we started on the journey. The first 100 feet were smooth and we mistakenly believed that we had chosen the path well... What awaited us were huge boulders where one had to grasp non-existent handholds and throw legs over and hoist up...A cave made only for small children and those who were not claustrophobic...Iron ladders and rungs? Sure, but up the sheer side of a cliff where any drop might be 30 feet! (Pat, but that is what a precipice is!)...Did I say that it had rained the night before and, because of large puddles and slippery surfaces, a perilous journey became even more dangerous?...And maybe the most dangerous of all? We had misjudged how much water we would need and brought two bottles for 5 people...A .8 mile hike up a cliff took us 3 hours and much sweat. Finally reaching the top after some very close and scary situations, we were dehydrated, agitated and tired. A group at the top lent us a bottled water and I realized how much our bodies and spirits needed this natural elixir to make it back down to the car without passing out!

Water, water, water…Thunder Hole and the power of water crashing against rock…Promises of a beautiful view of the Atlantic Ocean from the top of the Precipice…The danger and peril of navigating wet trails from an otherwise friendly (and needed) rain…And, water as nourishment and sustenance during a long and difficult hike…Many different images and definitions of H2O, some that wreck havoc and destruction on the earth (and our little trip!), others that signify beauty, health and life!

For anyone who has ever experienced a hike like this or who has practiced or played a sport in hot weather, the natural need for water becomes apparent. In fact, there is nothing that will quench our incredible thirst after a workout like a cool glass of water. As our family ventured to the top of the Precipice, our need for water became imperative. It was completely natural that our bodies craved water; it is when we no longer feel thirsty it becomes unnatural and our bodies unhealthy. That same thirst for water can be a symbol for our thirst for truth, for purpose and meaning, for God. It is completely natural for us to thirst for the spiritual because we are by nature spiritual beings! Saint Teresa of Jesus (also known as Teresa of Avila), in her Way of Perfection, expresses that image of water for the thirsty as our desire for God and all things spiritual.

In this life the soul will never thirst for anything more, although its thirst for things in the life to come will exceed any natural thirst that we can imagine here below. How the soul thirsts to experience this thirst! For it knows how very precious it is and, grievous though it be and exhausting, it creates the very satisfaction by which this thirst is allayed…one of the greatest favours He can bestow on the soul is to leave it with this longing, so that it has an even greater desire to drink of this water again.(1)

Saint Teresa's way of perfection in faith is to acknowledge that our soul is very naturally made to search out spiritual truth. She even likens spirituality to a 'favour,' a gift of God (like the water from the strangers at the Precipice) that we long for with all of our being. Being human, then, means to thirst for truth, to have questions and to seek out a deeper understanding of all things spiritual.

Pope John Paul II also shared this sentiment; our longing for God and all things spiritual was not a weakness but who we are naturally made to be. Peggy Noonan, in *John Paul the Great: Remembering A Spiritual Father*, comments on his beliefs:

> The pope believed that all of us, all of the human beings alive in the world right now, are a community of individuals who travel through history together. And

we travel with similar luggage. Each of us struggles through primary and essential questions that we cannot avoid once we reach or approach maturity. Why was I born? What is the meaning of life, and its purpose? Where and how can I find happiness? Why is life so full of pain and difficulty? How should we live, by what model or principles or arrangements? A great mystery embraces our lives, John Paul said. Then he added something that has been to me deeply inspiring: These questions we ask do not come only from your restless mind, and are not just products of your very human anxiety. They come from God. They are the beginning of the process by which you find him. God prompts them. He made you to ask. The questions are, in fact, a kind of preparation for God, a necessary preamble to the story he wants to write on your heart. (2)

Whew, it is kind of mind-boggling to think that the One some call "living water" is the same One who gives us a thirst for questions. Pope John Paul II knew through his faith and interactions with other people that we all thirst; but he didn't just stop there. In his claim that our desire for looking deeper comes from God, John Paul is saying that it is well and good.

Catholic Worker movement founder, Dorothy Day, was parched for truth and wisdom when she prayed. She had dappled in socialism (religion is the opiate of the people!) and anarchy, and strayed far from religion and God. Although her prayer was very often in acting for peace and justice, she found herself desiring a personal communication with Jesus, but sometimes doubted what she was doing. Her spiritual thirst and inner turmoil is described in Selected Writings of Dorothy Day, this time at age 25:

I am surprised that I am beginning to pray daily. I began because I had to. I just found myself praying. I can't get down on my knees, but I can pray while I am walking. If I get down on my knees I think, "Do I really believe? Whom am I praying to?" And a terrible doubt comes over me, and a sense of shame, and I wonder if I am praying because I am lonely, because I am unhappy..."But," I reason with myself, "I am praying because I am happy, not because I am

unhappy. I did not turn to God in unhappiness, in grief,
in despair-to get consolation, to get something from
Him. And encouraged that I am praying because I
want to thank Him, I go on praying. (3)

Dorothy Day desired a relationship with God but seemed to
second guess herself and her worthiness. It was natural for these
doubts to occur; something was happening deep within her spirit to
change her and strengthen her in prayer. She wanted to know more
and know Jesus in a deeper way.

A picture that makes sense to me concerning this thirsting for truth is one of a bucket
of water. The bucket is broken, though, having
a hole in the bottom (you might call it a 'holy
bucket.') No matter what goes in the bucket,
no matter what we put in to quench the thirst of
our soul, the water will always fall out the bottom. Material things (think of your last Christ-
mas list of desires...do you still use them?), fame, power, even intimacy in relationships (can any one person fill you completely?) will
never fill that bucket...unless we do some repairs to the hole by being
open and keeping the search for truth alive. We are made as buckets,
always trying to find ways to fill ourselves but never completely
succeeding...and this is the nature of who we are as spiritual beings,
as persons of faith! Philosopher Jean Paul Sartre once said that we
have a 'God-shaped hole in our lives' and only God can fill it!

Asking the tough questions and making a choice to have a
relationship with God, as Jane, a teenager from Minnesota implies, are
first steps in mending the hole:

I think that if you are a person of faith, you have to
question and doubt. God gave us the faith that we
have, but he also gave us the brains that we have.
God doesn't want us to blindly follow him, but to truly
choose to love him. Sometimes things happen in life
that we can't understand; this is when we doubt. {Jane,
Minnesota}

In *The Holy Longing*, Fr. Ron Rohlheiser writes that spirituality is ingrained in us as much as breathing. Spiritual questioning comes
when we naturally work through the deep stuff of life. He says,

Spirituality is not something on the fringes, an option
for those with a particular bent. None of us has a

choice. Everyone has to have a spirituality and everyone does have one, either a life-giving one or a destructive one…Long before we do anything explicitly religious at all, we have to do something about the fire that burns within us. What we do with that fire, how we channel it, is our spirituality….What shapes our actions is our spirituality. And what shapes our actions is basically what shapes our desire … Spirituality concerns what we do with desire.(4)

Author and educator Thomas Groome proposes that not only are we spiritual beings, but that this philosophy is found in all world religions. Because individuals long for the deeper things in life, every religion from Hindi to Buddhism to Islam to Judaism to Christianity possess common characteristics here:

Although life in the world may look very material, in fact it's deeply spiritual. What's more, the human spirit shares intimately in this Spirit Realm: it's our true home. For all the great religions, the Transcendent represents ultimate truth and goodness, justice and peace; thus, people should so live. (5)

Okay, so what does this mean for those who are in high school or finishing college or young adults in the workforce? While the images like buckets and water and life's longings may be universal, something might be happening at this time in your life as a young adult that further accentuates a thirst for truth. It would not be a surprise to you that developmentally, you are going through quite a bit right now. Over the last couple of years, not only has your body changed because of puberty, but hopefully you have grown emotionally, mentally and spiritually.

Has your family ever had work done on your house? We recently completed renovations on our basement, creating a space where we could entertain, relax and put the rest of our junk. During the carpentry and plumbing 'phase', the place was a mess. Drywall, tools, pipes, electrical materials, paint, and plenty of dust were the order of the day. It seemed as though one could not visualize the finished product with so much construction taking place.

While, we are all 'under construction,' high school and college years are particularly times of creation and also chaos. Physical changes, mental stretching, emotional roller coasters and, yes, even spiritual doubts and insights are all the norms of the day. It would probably be fairly easy to think about the physical developments that have happened to you over the last few years. You might even be able to pinpoint some major advancements in thought patterns (go calculus and physics!) or maturity in emotions. And yet, would it be so easy to think of the changes that you have gone through spiritually? And, if you are having some doubts about faith, do you see it as normal to your growth, as a natural part of who you are right now?

In his creatively titled book, Sometimes We Dance, Sometimes We Wrestle, long time youth ministry speaker and author Mike Carotta says that doubting in adolescent spirituality is just that: normal to growth and a natural part of who you are:

> Doubt plays a creative role within adolescent spiritu-
> ality. Since criticizing is a characteristic trait of ado-
> lescence, it naturally moves young people to doubt
> certain religious teachings and concepts, even regard-
> ing some of the mysteries of their faith. Critical think-
> ing, combined with a need for independence, results
> in spiritual doubting among adolescents. If handled
> well by the adult community, such doubting can result
> in a system of religious beliefs and moral values that
> the adolescent 'owns' and is willing to defend, even in
> the face of rejection from peers. (6)

Both Liz and Caitlin affirm this in their reflection essays con-
cerning their own times of doubt. For Liz, church teachings, God's will and why bad things happen to good people make her ask the tough questions. She considers those hesitations of her faith to be purely natural and even growth producing. She says:

> I think that doubt is just questioning something that's
> been taught or believed. There are a lot of different
> degrees of doubt. Personally when I doubt my faith, I
> do not think I necessarily doubt God, but more the
> church or in some circumstances His choices. Or my
> ability to deal with what He has handed me. But I do
> not feel these doubts make me unfaithful. I still con-
> sider myself a person of faith. Sometimes I question
> the importance of certain traditions that have been
> taught to us by the church. I question whether I can
> handle what God has handed me. I question why things
> happen and if it really is the right thing. If anything
> sometimes I think that these doubts strengthen my

faith, because it makes me question and dive further into my faith. {Liz, Maryland}

Caitlin also believes that her own current faith was made stronger because of doubt. During her confirmation preparations, she found that she was questioning not only her motives for being confirmed, but also her parent's decisions and the Catholic Church's teachings on a variety of issues. She writes:

> Even though, my first decision to not be confirmed confused everyone, in the end I grew stronger in my faith. I had learned more than I had ever before, even with all of the religious education classes I had taken in my life, I know that if I hadn't doubted my belief in Catholicism, that I would have not learned as much or gained anything through the experience. It was through doubt in my religion that I grew as much as I did. It turned out that I didn't really know much about Catholicism and my doubt was based on the little information I had. I needed to learn more, and I found a way to get the information I needed. I continue to believe that in order for someone to be truly strong in their religion, they have to question it. Questions lead to answers and explanations for misunderstandings and disbeliefs. As with all other times in life when we wish to learn; we must first question what we already know. {Caitlin, Washington, DC.}

As you can see with Caitlin and Liz (and probably tell in your own life), abstract thought, or the ability to think outside of the box and not just have blind faith in what others have told you, has very naturally kicked in now and you are developmentally able to ask the deeper questions and question the previously held truths. Some 'experts' like John Westerhoff say that your spirituality is in process from affiliative faith (faith of the emotions and those of your parents) to searching faith (everything comes under scrutiny, sometimes especially those beliefs of your parents!)

This is expected and ordinary, although it may seem anything but ordinary, so you can begin to form your own beliefs in a mature way. Ex-president Jimmy Carter, starting early in Sunday school and later in college with his buddies, maturely tackled the tough questions. Yet even as a child, I was dismayed to find myself becoming skeptical about some aspects of my inherited faith...what made it worse was that I thought I was the only person with such concerns. I felt guilty that I doubted what the preacher said and what my father taught me in Sunday school... Through it all, my worry over the doubts I felt about some Christian teachings continued, and my skepticism was somewhat heightened when I went away to college. I took part in the usual all night discussions with my freshman and sophomore classmates about big philosophical issues: Why was I created? What is the purpose of life? Who or what is God? We questioned everything, and we thought we were quite profound...Maybe some Christians never lack faith-they are the lucky ones. However, I don't know of anybody who has never had doubts about any aspect of the Christian faith...Perhaps we are afraid that opening the door to a little questioning might shake the foundation of our faith. But I came to realize that it is a mistake not to face our doubts courageously. We should be willing to ask questions, always searching for a closer relationship with God, a more profound faith in Christ. (7)

As Jimmy Carter implies, where you are right now is where you need to be. Asking the important questions, deciding who you are is just as important as choosing a college or deciding upon a career.

When 23 year old Jamie from New York heard that I was writing this book, she excitedly exclaimed that I must read a book she had recently discovered. She strongly recommended the national bestseller and landmark book, Quarterlife Crisis: The Unique Challenges of Life in your Twenties. Authors Alexandra Robbins and Abby Wilner (young adults themselves!) raise the issue of this being a time to struggle and search for truth:

"I know you asked for answers, but isn't this all about the questions we have? Isn't that the quintessential element of this period-questioning? It just varies by degree from person to person." (8)

Robbins and Wilner claim that the "quarterlife," like midlife, is a time of crisis of self, where the foundations laid previously in family and education are sometimes shaken, support systems are uprooted and the ego takes a beating. It is natural to not only question your faith but to question everything previously believed to be true. Andrea expresses this belief as well:

> Doubt is when one thinks within the "human" parameter and disregards the "God" parameter. Humans are taught to question everything, and believe nothing without proof. Faith is therefore contrary to what the human species has been taught over time. Faith in God requires us to believe something that has no tangible proof, something that is outside the "human" thought parameter. Therefore, because God gave humans the gift of free will, people, even the most devout, have the ability to determine what is true and what is not in this world. Yet doubting and losing faith altogether are two different things. Doubting is in fact a means to draw closer to God, and when one overcomes the doubt, the doubt gives way to truth and belief. So, yes, it is perfectly normal for a person of faith to question or doubt the basis of their faith. {Andrea, Minnesota}

Some adults find this time of questioning troubling and a sign of immaturity or even sin. Sandy, a 21 year old person from Texas, was told by her mom that doubting is a sin and the devil was behind it. Luckily, her youth minister's loving response of "Doubt is a sign of growth, that you are ready to go deeper" gave her not only a different perspective but an affirmation of hope.

I am sure that others have heard this mother's idea as well, coming from the traditional belief that our faith must be rock solid. To some people, doubt represents a crack in that rock. And yet, one top contemporary sociologist suggests that just the opposite is taking place.

> Peter Berger maintains that adolescents' passionate refusal to accept a 'comfortable settling down with half-truths' is a sign not of immaturity, but that the young person has reached a crucial decision point. (9)

Berger says that the decision here is what to do with 'intellectual passions of rebellion,' or using the gift of abstract thought to question authority. It is almost as if doubt is a companion to faith, a natural friend as we struggle and thirst for the answers to life's questions.

Reginald Blount, long-time youth minister and pastor, believes that all young people have seven spiritual yearnings (or thirsts) which will naturally cause them to seek profound truths. In Search of Living Waters: The Seven Spiritual Yearnings of Youth (10), Blount identifies the 'thirsts' of young people; Identity, intimacy, purpose, healing, mentoring, nurture, and courage. (In the interest of this book, I will adapt these and mesh intimacy, mentoring and nurture together.)

Identity, or the natural desire to know who you are (and Whose you are), is very difficult to pinpoint today in our world. In a very real way, we are caught up in accepting or tolerating every point of view and being open to everyone's story, so much so that we have a tough time identifying what we believe to be truth. As has been illustrated in credit card commercials, someone or something has stolen our identity and it is very hard to understand where we have come and who we are. It is complicated today to state in clear terms what we believe and feel, and the reasons we act. It is nearly impossible to proudly say how those beliefs and actions are different from others because of who we are. The thirst or yearning, then, is to discover what descriptions are on our ID card, that is, what makes us unique and special in spirit, mind, body and personality.

Intimacy, according to Blount, is the longing for relationships and ways to be connected. Although I will be writing about intimacy in the next chapter, it is too important as a thirst not to comment upon here. We all desire to be affirmed, supported, loved, even challenged by those who hold our very person in esteem. A recent but long-term study of premature babies showed that those who could not be held due to exposure to deadly germs did not have as confident of a self-image as those who were cuddled and touched. There was even evidence that babies given affection on a regular basis were healing at a quicker pace than those who were not!

Parker Palmer communicates this need for intimacy and connection as we ask deeper questions of spirit. He writes that we need other people in the travels of the soul for three reasons:

1. The journey toward inner truth is too taxing to be made solo; lacking support, the solitary traveler soon becomes weary or fearful and is likely to quit the road.
2. The path is too deeply hidden to be traveled without company: finding our way involves clues that are subtle and sometimes misleading, requiring the kind of discernment that can happen only in dialogue.
3. The destination is too daunting to be achieved alone: we need community to find the courage to venture into the alien lands to which the inner teacher may call us. (11)

Mentoring, which Blount sees as relationships to help us navigate the seas of doubt and questions, is a specific intimate relationship, a way to journey together towards 'inner truth.' There are those whom we consider close in our lives, whose nurturing and guidance help us to ask the questions in a compassionate and open environment. Although sometimes challenging and confrontational, mentors offer a safe place where we can discuss issues of the heart.

Purpose, another spiritual yearning that Blount suggests, is asking the questions "Why am I here?" and "What is the meaning of life?" Thomas Groome, professor at Boston College, claims that everyone at one time or another will ask the important questions. While some times of questioning may be more intense than others, it is who we are as spiritual beings. He says:

> Isn't it fascinating that every person tries somehow to 'make meaning' out of life, to have an outlook and a sense of purpose that holds things together? We search for meaning in spite of experiencing our mortality-that we get sick and die…and yet, though death is certain, we have a gut-level confidence that there is more to being human than eat, drink and be merry. In fact, there is much more to us than meets the eye…(12)

Stacie Orrico, a cross-over artist (Christian to all music tastes), came out with a search-for-meaning song that captures the essence of Groome's comments. There's Gotta Be More To Life (13) speaks volumes about our innate desire to look deeper, understand more fully, love more richly, and find meaning and purpose.

Healing, something that will be discussed in a future chapter on suffering, merits concern here as one of Reginald Blount's spiritual thirsts of young people. Blount says that young people have a need to be cured and revived from brokenness, rejection, ridicule, emotional and physical pain and oppression. Just glance at a magazine, TV show, internet site, my space or newspaper and you will see a broken world. It is a thirst that we all want quenched, a salve applied to our hurts so that we can function and thrive in the world. For example, psychologists believe that suicide is not so much a need to die as a desire not to live. According to studies, most people who are suicidal just don't want to hurt anymore. They want a cure, to be healed from their pain, to be relieved from that part which makes them consider death as an option.

Courage is the final spiritual longing that Blount raises. It is the ability to go against the crowd and stand out or be different. Some people use the symbol of a rubber band to express the courageous pulling away from truth that was taken for granted to now what is under suspicion. As you try to stretch the rubber band farther and farther away from its 'home base' (fingers, slingshots, etc), resistance and tension naturally occur. In fact, there are only a few options for a rubber band at this point: It either must go back to where it started or the object originally holding it has to let go or move towards it. If neither of these happens, the rubber band will break and cause pain to whoever holds it! It takes great courage to expand the rubber band but also bravery to come home when necessary. The stretching is natural, and must come to happen in order for rubber bands to fulfill a destiny as rubber band!

It is very interesting that Jesus seems to be the model for courage and this stretching tension. As Madeleine L'Engle writes:

> Read the Gospels. Read what this guy was really like. He had a strong personality, he told jokes, his friends were all the wrong people, he liked to go to parties. He didn't start a lepers' rights movement, he just healed lepers in his path. He was far more severe about people who were judgmental than he was about people who committed adultery. Love was always more important than anything else. All of his miracles were done on the Sabbath. God should have said, "Jesus, tone it down a bit. Be a little more tactful!" (14)

Jesus lived in tension, a tension that questioned previously held truths and had courage and love as its base. Remember that even Jesus tried to stretch the rubber band a bit, wandering off at age 12 to hang out in the temple, sitting among the teachers, listening to them and asking them questions. A very anxious (and angry?) Mary asks, "Son, why have you treated us like this? Your father and I have been anxiously searching for you." Jesus' response was "Why were you searching for me? Didn't you know I had to be in my Father's house?" (Luke 2:48-49) Now, while I am not suggesting that you respond to your parents this way after you come home late for curfew (unless you were at church; then you might stand a chance!), I think it is worthy of reflection that Jesus knew when to listen and ask questions, even if it meant being away from parents.

Whether the image be rubber bands, water, or buckets, then,

all humans (but particularly young people) possess an innate, natural longing to be more, understand more, desire more, question more. It is a gift of spirituality, a gift, if you will, from God that allows you to search more deeply for the riches that your life here offers.

Questions for Reflection:

1. Have you ever experienced a spiritual need or thirst?

2. Are doubts a gift/blessing or a curse? Why?

III. STRONG VOICES, TOUGH CHOICES

I had heard about this awesome college professor of cultural anthropology who, while making students think, was also very funny and engaging in his style. Since I was majoring in sociology and the course was required, I gladly enrolled. Who knew that it would be one of those college 'earthquake' moments that shook my faith to the core? ...

How solid has your faith foundation been growing up? Was your family an 'every-Sunday-and-then-some' family or a 'we'll-go-when-we-can' family? Was your family structure kind of chaotic and church (or faith) just wasn't a priority at all? Or was your family, like mine, Catholic to the core, with a faith and a God that was present throughout the day, in our decision making, in our relationships, in the ordinary, and, yes, in the Sacraments and in Scripture?

My own faith formation began by attending Catholic schools for twelve years (that's a lot of uniforms!). I was also involved in the Catholic Youth Organization (CYO), producing plays, helping with retreat weekends, serving on the youth leadership board, and growing closer to peers and adult volunteers. For three years in high school, I even worked for the local church as summer help and night watchman, sometimes clocking 70 hours per week during non-school seasons!

I will show you what someone is like who comes to me, listens to my words, and acts on them. That one is like a man building a house, who dug deeply and laid the foundation on rock; when the flood came, the river burst against that house but could not shake it because it had been well built. But the one who listens and does not act is like a man who built a house on the ground without a foundation. When the river burst against it, it collapsed at once and was completely destroyed. (1) (Luke 6:46-49)

Like a house built on rock, my faith foundation was probably better than most. I mean, I had family and friends who were (are) very close to God and each other in faith. I was active at the church and really felt like I had a more personal relationship with God. So, how could I possibly have a flood hit my well-founded house? How could I possibly have 'earthquake' moments so soon after this great high school experience?

For my freshman and sophomore college years, I decided to attend the local community college. This saved money and gave me the chance to test the waters before transferring to a college farther from home. During this time, I became painfully aware that my support system had changed. No longer was there an active 'youth group' model nor a strong Catholic high school with which I was affiliated. In fact, since I was going to a public school for the first time, I was in culture shock. What do you mean 'there is no God?' Do people really believe that? I was confronted, maybe for one of the first times, with things that I had previously held to be absolute truth. My close friends and I decided to form a young adult group at church which became very active and a very positive way to support each other.

I transferred to a Catholic college in my junior year, excited and ready to keep growing in the faith that I had experienced at my church. And yet, transferring was extremely difficult...I had to live off campus the first semester and dealt with pangs of loneliness and pain at being away from everything that was familiar and family-iar. When I did move to the dorms, I was struck by the contrast in Christian values that existed. My first roommate was either out at all hours of the night 'visiting the female persuasion' (his words!) or heavily partying, or, worse yet, had brought people back to the room to do one or the other!

And so, I was ready for the convictions of Catholic teaching in class and began my second semester with the security that this cultural anthropology class, amongst others, would build up that foundation of faith that I needed. Sure enough, Professor M., the well-loved cultural anthropology professor from the beginning of this chapter, was entertaining, funny, and caring. He awakened in all of us energy for studying groups of people and how their own belief systems and moral codes impacted our own. He motivated and inspired us to think deeply and ask questions about a wide range of subjects and issues that we had never asked before.

Sounds like an ideal class, right? It was in many ways, for it challenged me to begin making religion and faith my own, to begin focusing not on what I believe but why I have come to accept certain things about my faith. Is there a God, and, who is God? What is there besides being Catholic and why are Catholics owners of the truth?

Why are humans on this earth? What is our purpose? Are there absolute truths in life or are they just made up by groups of people? What is really right? What is wrong? Who am I to push my beliefs on someone else?

What made this class confusing was the fact that Professor M was a self-proclaimed atheist. Huh? Wait...I liked this guy! He was caring and challenging and passionate about his work. He got me a job at a department store as a security guard so I could make money during the holidays! I stopped in his office often to shoot the breeze and we could talk deeply about so many things! But he didn't believe in God...I had to take a second look at why I believed what I believed and this, coupled with some other philosophy courses that raised similar issues (and my less than perfect living situation) brought me to a rather intense period of doubt, which I believe I had to go through to be the person (of God) that I try to be now!

STRONG VOICES, TOUGH CHOICES

Besides the ideology of an atheist, there are those voices who will tell you that there are no absolutes, that anything goes. There are INNER VOICES and OUTER VOICES and also SILENCES where it seems as though there are no voices speaking at all, only a void or moments of solitudes when one must decide what to do themselves. In each of these instances, a person must decide how to listen and what or whom to listen to.

INNER VOICES

Whenever I write these two words, I envision someone hearing voices in their head, signaling that all may not be right upstairs! And yet, inner voices are very subtle and some seem to make sense. They say things like, "Don't buy into everything you hear." OR "I want to get ahead in life." OR "I have to look out for myself." OR "My faith and beliefs tell me not to do this." OR "I'm good enough, strong enough, handsome enough, smart enough." OR (you get the idea). The voices could be well-thought out over a period of time or completely impulsive, habitual or once in a lifetime, completely selfless or constantly selfish. Some inner voices motivate us, inspire us, call us to take risks and chances or pull back away from harm, and stretch us to grow and change. (One might even consider some of these voices to be from God!)

Robert writes about this inner voice:

...Nevertheless, questions about my identity and my life's purpose disturbed me deeply. College and career decisions hung over my head. Depression had set in, and my faith no longer seemed enough to overcome the insecurity and inner sadness I was encountering in my life. I believed in a God that heard my mumbles and sighs and occasional thanks, but I lost the intimate connection I used to feel. My faith had become stale, I felt little emotional stability, and less and less about life seemed certain. I began to think more skeptically. Does God really hear me? Has society just made God up over the past four thousand years? "Why, God, can't I hear you more clearly? If you want me to serve you, then tell me what to do! Otherwise, I'm going to give up." {Robert, Kentucky}

Some inner voices shame us, discourage us, guilt us, mislead us, call us to take dangerous risks or go towards harm, and want us to grow complacent in what is comfortable. Some inner voices might say, "I am too fat and don't need to eat at all for a few days." OR "I must party every weekend or I won't have any fun" OR "I have to have a boy or girlfriend or I won't be happy." The voices are so powerful and loud as to be addictive, where one feels no longer in control of their lives and something or someone else totally takes over. Drug and alcohol abuse, possessive relationships, eating disorders, depression, anxiety, and more all seem to overwhelm us so that healthy choices about listening to these voices are few and far between.

OUTER VOICES
Aside from the powerful inner voices, there are oh so many voices vying for our attention outside of us. As children, we were told not to use our outside voices inside but few were prepared how to deal with all of the outside voices there are in the world!

1. The Voice of Cultural Norms:
A.) Entertainment and Media has never been so accessible, blatant and crude as it is now. Not only is it easy to be entertained by computer, cell phone or TV today, but the voice messages coming out are pretty blatant. If you are 'entertained' by 'porn,' it is available. If you happened to miss a show because of another commitment, here it is on TiVo. If you are dying to hear the latest music from your favorite

band, die no more. Instead, download onto your IPOD! And the voices of entertainment and media are not innocent voices because these voices come with a price tag (and I am not speaking about your soul!) Billions of dollars are spent by young people every year on entertainment and the media industry wants those dollars to continue being squandered. So, media moguls find out how to market for those dollars and create new and improved technology, TV shows, communications devices and computer programs to increase Christmas lists and shopping needs. Images that excite, anger, confuse or attempt to satisfy your curiosity are designed by people whose motives are not always completely innocent. And yet, these voices are some of the most powerful, especially when it comes to how we are suppose to relate to each other!

B.) Say the word intimacy today and some would get embarrassed or begin laughing or conjure up images of lingerie and private places. I saw a court of law show that deals with divorces. A man was on the witness stand and was being questioned rather aggressively by his ex-wife's lawyer. The lawyer grilled him by asking, "Isn't it true that on April 29, you were not only intimate with one woman, but with two?" The man burst into tears and confessed. Hold on, isn't the definition of intimacy all about closeness and the depth of spirit which is innermost to our being? (look it up!) Have we deafened our ears by listening to voices telling us that the best way to get close to someone is to have sex with them? True intimacy, true closeness with another person is about three things: a process or a journey of discovery and growing in love; a person with strengths and weaknesses, hopes and dreams, joys and struggles, a body and mind and soul; and a spiritual presence which mutes all of those other voices about intimacy and what we consider important.

C.) The best things in life aren't things at all! Given the mega-malls and emphasis on shopping, especially around the holidays, I guess some of us believe otherwise! Commercialism doesn't just tell us what to buy, but that buying is important and you will miss out if you are not out buying! Stores begin advertising for some holidays months earlier and put sales up for the next holiday before the current one is even over! Items from the internet are easy to find and buy, all from the comfort of your room (until you see the credit card bill!). Thomas Groome cautions about this:

> "Being convinced that the world is meaningful should
> not make us naïve about countersigns…besides truth
> there is falsehood…The dominant attitude of society

is that our worth depends on what we do, possess, or achieve. Christian faith, by contrast, holds that the worthwhileness of life-like its meaningfulness-does not depend on our efforts alone."(2)

D.) The best things in life really have nothing to do with things. It has everything to do with matters of the heart and soul. And think about this…where some of us are looking for the current fads in clothes or the hottest trends, others in this world are looking for fresh water and the next piece of bread. How did we as people of privilege get so lucky in life's lottery? Or are we really lucky? Does this voice of consumerism make us happy or just make us want more?

E.) I'm free to do what I want any ol' time. A popular song from another time but still relevant today! The voice that speaks this message, it seems, is designed to protect our individual rights. As people of the United States, we cherish our rights: freedom of speech, religion, voting to name a few. But, are we free to do anything at all? Doesn't our need to be free sometimes impede other's needs? Are all freedoms good for us? When our freedom of expression hurts someone, are we all really that free? When our freedom of religion means that we disregard someone else's beliefs, is this freedom? Some wise person once said that the key to life is not finally being independent and free, but to be interdependent and see not only our own rights but our responsibilities to the people around us.

F.) I can't get no satisfaction, but I try…Oh yes, classic rock! I had a conversation with a young friend of mine who is in college. He said that 'all he wanted to be was happy and would try in anyway to make it happen.' Sure enough, he was involved in drugs and sleeping around, trying to find that happiness, even for a brief time. Was he happy? Our culture makes it seem like becoming happy is wrapped up in prestige or power or popularity or getting high on material goods or substances or sexual activity. Anyone who has ever tried to find happiness in this way will eventually express the superficiality of this voice, which pales in comparison to the satisfaction that comes from John 10:10

"I have come that you might have life, and have it abundantly." Hmmm…Temporary happiness or the joy of a lifetime?

2. The Voice of Advancements In Science and Technology

One of the greatest pressures facing young people in new settings is the insecurity of not knowing anyone and not having anyone know you. We all desire a sense of belonging to a group where we can feel comfortable and at home. Maybe this is why all of us spend so much time and energy with 'things of technology.' Maybe that is why the voice of electronics is so loud today! If "IM" to you means "I AM HOOKED", you belong to a group addicted to this new form of instant messages of communication. If you are a prisoner of your cell, (get it?), you belong to your friends and family 24/7. If your 'face book' or 'my space' is a show-all, tell-all profile, you belong to a group that find it important to share important things, sometimes even with strangers. If the "e" in email means "everyday" or "every minute," you belong to a cyber-community that has gotten so big that it has made billionaires! And yet, all of these are able to be communicated without ever leaving your home. Just a question: Does this contribute to or take away from a sense of true belonging? I have noticed over the years that knowing someone is not the same as knowing about someone. In other words, we can 'talk' to people using technology but that is not the same as sitting down facing to face and spending time with that person. And, one more thing, I think this is true for our relationship with Jesus, too. We can know about him but, until we truly meet him facebook to facebook, I mean, face to face in the Sacraments, Scripture, or in a person who is poor, then we really don't know him. In our quest for knowledge and advancements in science and technology, are we missing who Jesus really was(is)? Martin Luther King, decades ago, commented on this:

> The great tragedy is that Christianity failed to see that it had the revolutionary edge. You don't have to go to Karl Marx to learn how to be a revolutionary. I didn't get my inspiration from Karl Marx; I got it from a man named Jesus, a Galilean saint who said he was anointed to heal the broken-hearted. He was anointed to deal with the problems of the poor. And that is where we get our inspiration. And we go out in a day when we have a message for the world, and we can change this world and we can change this nation. (3)

I was talking to a young man in Maryland who thought that intelligent people don't believe in God. James said that science is intelligence and that, since there is no scientific way to prove God, he wanted nothing to do with it. Yet, Ryan, an extremely intelligent University of Rochester college student majoring in physics and calculus, is excited about recent developments in science. Although he has really been questioning his faith since he left home last year, Ryan believes that new theories concerning dimensions of time and spaces suggest to him and others that a higher power, God, can indeed be proven soon. He has also heard about a well-known physics professor who states that there is evidence for the existence of God. One only has to look at the 'perfect' conditions that were met to bring the earth into creation (and keep it running!) to surmise that a Supreme Being is a reality.

Science and empirical data would make our faith easier, or would it be faith at all? There has been a strong voice which states that beliefs about evolution, biology, physics, psychology and other fields leave no room for the existence of God and, therefore, all of the religions that hold this belief are in error. Great controversies and conflicts arise in public school settings, fields of science and technology, and politics which indicate that, to be a believer in God and to put faith in things other than empirically-based is a waste of time and thought. And yet, the idea that science and technology will solve all of our problems and make us happy has not been realized over the years. Indeed, it seems as though we are even more alienated, each of us at our laptops or in our bedrooms, getting readily accessible information on any topic or anonymously conversing about very personal issues. Science and technology fall short and are unable to deliver any kind of perfect world or utopian happiness. What is missing? Maybe the missing link is a sense of mystery or awe at the unknowable and personally belonging to someone or something special. While I do not argue with the power of empirical data, I do find myself placing a different emphasis on it as a person of faith, much like Bono (U2 fame) when he had a revelation after falling asleep in St. Patrick's Cathedral in Dublin. He explains it in this way:

> It dawned on me for the first time, really. It had dawned on me before, but it really sank in: the Christmas story. The idea that God, if there is a force of Love and Logic in the universe, that it would seek to explain itself is amazing enough. That it would seek to explain itself and describe itself by becoming a child born in straw poverty...a child. I just thought: Wow! Just the poetry...Unknowable love, unknowable power, describes itself as the most vulnerable...There it was. I was sitting there...tears came down my face, and I saw the genius of this, utter genius of picking a particular point in time and deciding to turn on this...love needs to find form, intimacy needs to be whispered. To me, it makes sense. It's actually logic. It's pure

logic. Essence has to manifest itself. It's inevitable.
Love has to become an action or something concrete.
It would have to happen. There must be an incarna-
tion. Love must be made flesh. (4)

The spirit and the logical meet in a stable in Bethlehem. For
Bono, it may not be the most scientific awareness, but it made perfect
sense, faith seeking understanding if you will. Scientists who believe
like Bono, in an active and loving God, will have a slightly different
interpretative of data and 'logic' than those who love 'pure science.'

3. The Voice of Significant Others:
I think that parents and family in general provide
one's means to true freedom...placing myself in a
world and a story bigger than myself. (5)

Do you agree or disagree with this statement by Andrea, a
young adult from Portland, Oregon? How much of an influence are
parents and family to your faith when you are away at school or living
at home? Where on the 'faith line' do your parents and family lie?
Professed atheists or apathetics, practicing Catholics or perfect Christians, your parents have and will continue to wield a strong influence
on you.
I remember my college years as similar to living in two worlds:
the world of having to wake up for class on my own time and study
when and how I needed and the world of curfews and letting my parents know where I was going and what church service I was attending. Although my parents did treat me as a young adult, there were
times when the War of the Sprankle Worlds was sometimes fought. I
tested curfew limits and my dad was waiting for me. I made and spent
money sparingly but was asked to be more accountable. Still, they
were the stable influence as I was hearing other voices that allowed
me to question not only my faith but many different aspects of my life.
How about you? It is not just whether your parents are 'cool' about
your independence...what truths do they speak about who you are or
how you are responsible? What positive ways might you be changing
or growing as a person that may or may not be in line with their views?
The ever-serene and ever-insightful Mister Rogers, TV personality
and guru of child development, spoke words of wisdom, not only about
our parents, but all who have gone before us:
Each generation, in its turn, is a link between all that

has gone before and all that comes after. That is true genetically, and it is equally true in the transmission of identity. Our parents gave us what they were able to give, and we took what we could of it and made it part of ourselves. If we knew our grandparents, and even our great-grandparents, we will have taken from them what they could offer us, too. All that helped to make us who we are. We, in our turn, will offer what we can of ourselves to our children and their offspring. (6)

Parents, grandparents, even adults like coaches and teachers can impact us by what they offer, either positively or negatively. I spoke with a college athlete one time who said that his coach ran his life! During football season, there was not enough time to breathe, let alone study or hang with friends! This particular coach demanded three practices a day, a rigorous training schedule and much travel to away games. It seemed to this young man that his greatest influence were his coach and his teammates. While sports taught him discipline, belonging and the ability to reach goals, he missed what he called 'normal life' of sitting at his desk and studying or going to church on a regular basis or even partying in his dorm on a Thursday or Friday. In high school or college, 'who you are' is really shaped by these people we call "coaches." A coach can be all about winning or about playing your best (or somewhere in between). A coach can say that missing any practice means not playing in a game or can be flexible about other commitments, especially those of a religious nature. There are coaches that have no problem saying a prayer in the locker room or profanity on the field (and some who do both!) All in all, coaches and all significant adults have the ability to be yet another voice of influence, sometimes affecting our faith, the way we see and the way we act on it. Robert speaks about being indirectly challenged by a high school teacher:

> At this point in my life, especially during senior year, I found myself exposed to many new ways of thinking. As my intellect developed, I realized how many contrasting ideas about life exist and was over- whelmed attempting to sort them out. Postmodernism and I were not quick friends. Gradually, however, I learned to accept the reality of our world, and the liberating (to an extent, I think) ambiguity even exhilarated me at

times. In world religions class, I found myself ready to convert to almost any of the faiths we studied; they all seemed truthful.

In my Christian Lifestyles class, my teacher seldom mentioned Christ. When he did, it was usually an offhand joke or a reference to an objective study dismantling traditional myths about Jesus' life. "What?" I would respond, "Jesus wasn't born in the manger?" "Nazareth?—I thought he was born in Bethlehem!" Sometimes his skeptical approach to religion offended me, but now that the class is over, I'm glad my faith doesn't waver regarding simple facts like where Jesus was born... Though I think an approach that better recognizes the truth found in the Church would have benefited our skeptical class, I'm thankful my teacher challenged me to become more authentic and less fundamental in my faith. What I wanted was a class that reinforced my faith—not shook it—but perhaps that's not what I most needed. God's ways sure are higher than mine, and I'm coming to see how. {Robert, Kentucky}

The demands and ideologies of teachers and other adults present, including my professor at the beginning of the chapter and Robert's class above may also greatly impact how we view our world and spirituality. Other significant adults, such as Andrea's day care provider, inadvertently caused Andrea to get confused and begin doubting:

When I was younger, I used to go to a Christian home daycare service, and the daycare provider, Nancy, would teach us about God. I remember that on one particular day she was teaching us about the Creation stories in Genesis. I became really confused when she said that in the beginning there was nothing except darkness and God. I recall sitting outside on the swing thinking how weird and lonely that that must have been for God and I doubted if that were even possible, for how could there be nothing in the midst of nothing. {Andrea, Minnesota}

And what about your friends? A young woman came home from a summer of church events (a leadership conference and a mission trip to name a few), and was at first discouraged to find that, while her own values systems had changed, her friends' had not. She felt that she had grown so much from these experiences and really wanted nothing to do with the petty fights, gossip and backstabbing that had encompassed her current circle of friends. In her heart and soul, she knew that she might have to make some difficult decisions if she was going to be faithful to what had deeply affected her spirit during the summer. I don't need to tell you how much power and pressure these 'friendly' voices have over all of us. They can be forces for positive change and growth but can many times tear us down.

Friendships that become possessive or exclusive of others or demeaning can tear a hole in our lives. And friendships that are life-giving and selfless and inclusive (welcoming of others) can be the stuff of life! How much of an influence has your circle of friends been to you, your beliefs, and your growth? When friendships change because of transitions (like college), principles or interests, what can we learn?

Finally, religious leaders and spiritualities may be loud voices that touch or trouble your soul. While many of these voices are altruistic and authentic, there are those voices who will speak out of manipulation or personal motivations and the need for power, prestige, and other selfish gain. In short, the messenger becomes more important than the actual message. Jesus said that we will know people by their fruits, and, although some lifestyles and teachings may seem sweet and 'fruitful,' only time and careful scrutiny will tell. Distrust about a particular church or doctrine may be fostered because we experience humans making mistakes or committing grave sins or betraying trusts or making rigid rules concerning dogma or morality which we don't understand. Certainly, there have been voices within churches and other religions that have been less than compassionate and which raise questions of hypocrisy or even abuse of power.

Still, the voices of religious structures and formal institutions are strong ones, calling us to belonging and community that is at the core of who we are. Caitlin became disenchanted with the Catholic faith and looked around for an appropriate place to vent her disbeliefs. She felt deeply that having a problem with the dogmas of the Catholic Church meant that she had become faithless. She writes:

I was in tenth grade and I was already registered for confirmation classes at my church because it seemed to be the natural path. But every time I learned more about Catholicism, the more I disagreed. It was not all of Catholicism I disagreed with, just certain parts. The more I heard things that I did not understand, the more I was confused as to what I was supposed to do. I don't think it was one specific thing that initiated the doubt I was having. I was in high school, and most would figure that as a teenager, I had a natural tendency to want to be different and rebel. I was sure that this was not a case of rebellion, and I did not want my parents to think it was. That's what made it so hard for me to decide what to do.

For the most part, I thought that I should keep quiet and not tell anyone that I was having second thoughts. No one would want to hear that a tenth grader wanted to question the authority of Catholic teachings. For a few months, I just went along with things and did everything that I would if I was certain I wanted to be confirmed. But after a while, things started to get to me. From the time and effort that I had to put into being confirmed to the uncertainty inside of me, I was distraught. One day, I finally braved my parents and told them that I no longer wanted to be confirmed a Catholic. My parents did as any parents would; they worried about me and wanted to figure out why I had suddenly gone astray. Up until that day, I had been an active youth in the church. I was an altar server and I participated in activities held by the Catholic Youth Ministry team, like "Lunches to the Homeless," and I seemed to enjoy my faith and attending mass. No one saw it coming.

On the other hand, there are also voices who will tell you that you can pick between religions and ideologies just as if you were in the great cafeteria of life. This religious relativism (everything is alright and nothing is absolute) pervades our society and its voice speaks loudly to overshadow any real truth! In the R & R cafeteria, whatever you are hungry for and tastes good is there for the taking!

There is one more thing about religious relativism voices and the truth. It seems to me that many young people are not only search-ing for THE TRUTH but are sure that TRUTH does exist. Sure, there are developments in science (the world is really round and the earth is not the center of the universe!), medicine and other fields that seem to rock our comfortable faith worlds for awhile and there are 'truths' that have gone the wayside because someone proved some-thing else. Sure, there are academics who believe that religion is dead and secular humanism alive and well. Sure, there are those who think that, if it ain't intellectual enlightenment, it ain't worth a hill of beans (ain't is used intentionally!) Sure, there are New Age followers who, through crystals and meditation, believe that one can find the 'God-within.' Sure, there are some controversial novels about the hidden gospels like The Da Vinci Code that seem to shake what we have believed.

And yet, young people seem to want to believe in a God, in a spiritual world and in spirituality in general (maybe not so much estab-lished religion for some, but definitely spiritual matters!) Young people seem to want to believe in TRUTH. Maybe a way to look at it is that Truth does exist and realizing that the little truths of our lives (and our faith) are still unwritten or being revealed. In the article True For You, But Not True For Me, Sean McDowell tells about an experience that Dr. Francis Beckwith (professor of philosophy at Baylor University), had with a skeptical student in his ethics class.

> One day she asked, "Dr. Beckwith, why is truth so important?" After thinking for a moment he gave this reply, "Well, would you like the true answer or the false one?" In other words (McDowell writes), the very question assumed the existence, the knowability, and the importance of truth." (7)

It seems as though this student asked the question of Dr. Beckwith, unconsciously feeling that truth is real, achievable and es-sential to who we are as human beings. The voices in this world who question moral and/or spiritual truth spend much time and energy doing so, but their very questioning implies a search for that truth!

SILENCES...

Depending on who you are, sometimes the scariest voices are those which make no sound. While prayerful silence many times al-lows for peaceful reflection and personal perspective changes, there is fear in being away from those voices (family, friends, church) that has provided a solid system of influence. After asking four college students why they have doubts and what is most difficult about keeping their faith, they commented as one, "The greatest influence in our doubting was being away from home for the first time. The most difficult part is being away from your home base." When I asked them to explain this, they each said that they had to learn the hard way that no one would make them go to church or pray or decide what lifestyle they would live…it was up to them. The voice they would have to listen to was either their conscience (hopefully formed by that time) or the memory of voices from their past.

Since there is not always an established community at various times in our lives, college included, this encounter with 'the real world' can be troubling and lonely. In describing a "Quarterlife Crisis," the authors (Robbins and Wilner) explain a similar sentiment:

> But if the questioning becomes constant and the barrage of doubts never seem to cease, twentysomethings can feel as if it is hard to catch their breath, as if they are spiraling downward. Many times the doubts increase because twentysomethings think it is abnormal to have them in the first place. No one talks about having doubts at this age, so when twentysomethings do find that they are continuously questioning themselves, they think something is wrong with them. (8)

This feeling of 'going it alone' makes the silence feel oppressive, the important self-reflection and personal quiet seem like an enemy. Finally, if 'all is quiet on the spiritual front' is accompanied by a perceived freedom to engage in risky behaviors like excessive partying or promiscuous sex, (because of our need to fill the quiet chasm with loud noises), we can tend to spiral deeper and deeper into guilt, isolation and despair.

One more thing about silences…Sometimes we may be given a message that we miss because we are looking for some great sign. Gene Monterastelli, in How To Save The World and Retire, writes about an experience about looking for God to answer a prayer.

> At one point a number of years ago, I was feeling very unsettled. I was trying to figure out what would be the next thing I would create…In all of this, I had been looking for guidance in prayer…After a few weeks, it was becoming obvious that I had not been paying attention. The signals were getting blatant and, what was worse, I was still not getting the message.(9)

Gene then goes on to identify a friend, a woman at a movie theatre, and a guy who was homeless, all who were 'messengers of God' to him, all who God used to answer his prayer. He says that his life (including his sense of quiet reflection and prayer) would be different if he saw everyone as a messenger of God. When God comes in the whisper of the wind (1 Kings 19: 11-12), this should alert all of us to listen more closely and quietly for the voice of God.

In conclusion, inner and outer voices plus the sounds of silence sometimes cause us to question what we have previously held dear and true to our hearts. These voices can be deafening or defeating, hushed or hurried, ever-changing and a steady barrage, affirming or crippling. The important skill to learn is the ability to be open and listen to the right or true voices.

Questions for Reflection:

1. Who or what are the voices that grab your attention? (Inner and outer)

2. Write 3 voices to which you should listen more? Less?

IV. SUFFERING & WHITE FLOWERS:

Kevin was a young man I got to know when I was working as a high school campus minister. Kevin was involved in everything: His charisma made him a sure win for student government and, ultimately, student body president in senior year. His athletic skills assured him a position on the nationally ranked football and lacrosse teams, and, because of his leadership and passion, he was quickly made captain of each. His desire to work in campus ministry on retreats and prayer services, though, is where we really crossed paths. Kevin was obviously engaged in his faith and brought it into every aspect of his life. Through his own spirituality, he inspired other people to make God first. My relationship with this dynamic young man made his early death at 19 years old even more difficult to understand.

It seems Kevin was coming out of his fraternity house at UNC (where he was again excelling in lacrosse and academics) and was shot by an ex-law student who had gone ballistic. There was no rhyme or reason about this tragedy...but Kevin was yet another victim of the violence that seems to pervade our society.

I pulled up at the funeral home down the street from Kevin's old high school and was immediately struck by the line. Winding around three blocks, it was filled with friends and family in obvious pain and shock, everyone trying to make sense out of something that will really never make sense. As I waited, watching, praying and talking, I noticed something. Big football and lacrosse players, their field machismo gone for the moment, were crying and hugging each other. They were also looking for answers. "Why Kevin?" "Why did this have to happen?" And the inevitable: "Why did God allow this to happen?"

Kevin, Creighton, Tommy, Jackie, Ryan, Christen, John, JT, Tara, Colleen & Erin, Kevin...Such is the litany of some young people I have known in my ministry who have died too early from accidents, overdoses, violence, terminal illness, and natural disaster (Colleen & Erin were killed when a tornado ripped through the University of Maryland campus, hurling their car over a building). It is one of the toughest parts of my job to help others (and myself) say goodbye and grieve for a life that ended prematurely. My personal feelings of shock, anger, frustration, confusion and sadness are shared by so many others when early death slaps us in the face and out of our comfortable existence.

In a world filled with situations like this, it is easy to ask these questions, harder still, it seems to find answers. Terrorists strike and thousands of people are killed. Tsunamis hit and hundreds of thousands loses their lives, their homes, their families. Wars break out; some planned over time by manipulators of power and others the result of festering conflict or corrupt politicians. A person who is homosexual is beaten to death by those who consider him too different or strange. A woman is sexually harassed in the workplace and management wants her to forget about it or risk losing her job.

Abuse, plague, gang violence, school shootings, hurricanes, and more. Overwhelming hopelessness, the darkness of a culture out of control. Why God? How can this be part of a loving plan? If you are all powerful, why don't you stop this, protect your people? If you are all loving, why must there be so much hate? If you are all knowing, couldn't you have created a world without these crazy things going on? Where are you, God? Poet John Geoffrey Arthur Morgan reflects on these sentiments when he writes:

> There cannot be a God. The God I worship should love me, yet I'm afflicted by pain, driven insane by heaven above. Where is Satan? Where is God? The antithesis becomes the thesis. Is there a God to protect me? I have meditated and prayed yet suffer more pain from the one I love.

It is possible to experience an uncertainty not just about God's existence, but God's motives with human beings. The poet's underlying question, "Is God good or evil?" suggests a lack of confidence in the all loving God of Judaism and Christianity. Is God really somehow (in a warped way) to blame for the tragedies and trials of this world?

While searching through the internet about 'doubting faith,' I found a myspace blog which echoes this feeling. This person's spiritual journey (and journal) seems to mirror John G.A. Morgan's poem, oozing angst, pain, the innate desire for things to be different and for God to be present. I'm sure that you will recognize the poetic license this blog writer takes with grammar and punctuation!

Current Mood: Confused. Well, I wrote this song is sort of about to completely different things but its one song. It's a little rough cause I have not edited it at all. Tell me what u think.

"I am doubting faith and confidence and wondering what I should do I see all the atrocities but somehow keep thinking of you. It's a world of war, a world of peace is all I wanted to all the things done in your name what a f***ing shame. I don't know what I believe no more wish life was a easy bore but somehow I keep thinking of you can't start again, I can't begin but still remembering you." {RCM}

RCM speaks from the heart and, I believe, from the darkness of the soul, longing for a better world, longing also for God to step in. It is probable that, like these two reflections, each person will at some point question "God, exactly what are you doing here? Why do you allow this to happen? Why must we experience such loss and pain while we are alive?" I mean, isn't this the stuff of searching? Haven't writers for thousands of years been asking the same questions in one way or another? The human authors of the Hebrew Scriptures, under the inspiration of the Holy Spirit, toiled with it in the story of Job, where an innocent man loses everything and is encouraged to leave God behind.

Thomas Groome summarizes the dilemma of the problem of evil, particularly in the Book of Job, when we writes:

Let's admit immediately that believers-theists-have no convincing explanation for evil and suffering, much as atheists are stumped by goodness and love. Even the Bible explicitly recognizes that suffering is beyond human ken. Although Job is ever our hero for questioning God about it, his eventual sentiments are: "I have dealt with great things that I do not understand; things too wonderful for me, which I cannot know." (Job 42:3) (1)

Others have brought up this ultimate concern in their own wresting with suffering. Thomas, in his pain over the death of his friend and teacher, Jesus, does not even believe his fellow apostles when they say they have seen the Risen Lord.

I will not believe until I see the nail marks in his hands

and put my finger where the nails were, and put my
hand in his side. (John 20:25)

Camus' Nobel Prize winning classic, The Plague, raises the dilemma of widespread suffering of innocent people in the Middle Ages
and the difficulty of coming to terms seeing any God as good. Father
Paneloux, who attempts to bring solace and hope in a world gone mad
by the plague, sermonizes but, Dr. Rieux, who has been in the thick of
disease, suffering and death, and is in a crisis of faith, is skeptical:

> Indeed, we were all up against the wall that plague
> had built around us, and in its lethal shadow we must
> work out our salvation. He, Father Paneloux, refused
> to have recourse to simple devices enabling him to
> scale that wall. Thus he might easily have assured
> them that a child's sufferings would be compensated
> for by an eternity of bliss awaiting him. But how could
> he give that assurance when, to tell the truth, he knew
> nothing about it? For who would dare to assert that
> eternal happiness can compensate for a single
> moment's human suffering? He who asserted that
> would not be a true Christian, a follower of the Mas-
> ter who knew all the pangs of suffering in his body
> and soul. (2)

Certainly, history has many examples of pain and suffering
but, in the past 100 years (even any recent 10 days!), we are faced
with the problem of evil and the God of love in our world. Two world
wars with atrocious acts of evil and death (some say a third is around
the corner), terrorism and tyranny, absolute power absolutely corrupt-
ing political structures and politicians, natural disasters that seem all
but natural to those who inhabit the earth, and new lists of suffering
and death that must be updated weekly and daily. And personal suffering, too, as is evidenced by Jane's essay:

> I can't name a particular time because there has never
> really been a big moment when I didn't know, just
> small bumps along the path. Most of the time when I
> doubt God it is when I am suffering or when I am
> hurting in someway. I am usually trying to figure out
> why God would allow that to happen to me, then I
> wonder if there is even a God. I think a lot of people
> do the same thing-doubt when they are hurting. I re-

alize that I the time that we should cling to God more, to help us deal with our hurts. I am getting better at trusting God and like the Casting Crown song says "I will praise you in the storm" {Jane, Minnesota}

And yet, like Jane in her last sentence, there are those who suffer greatly but seem to rise above the suffering. There are those who survive unspeakable ordeals and then speak words of hope and assurance to others. There are those whose own trials make our own pale in comparison, but they hold on to their sanity and faith and belief in the good of God and others. Who are these people and how is this possible? On closer scrutiny, what secrets do their lives, their attitudes, their spiritualities reveal? I believe that these qualities can be summed up in 3 words: attitude, awareness, action.

Attitude: Hope amidst hopelessness

We were warned to prepare the young people we took to World Youth Day in Cologne, Germany that part of our pilgrimage would be to Dachau, a World War II concentration camp near Munich. So, there we were at an iron gate where thousands upon thousands of people passed through only 60 years ago on their way into a nightmare. Human beings whose 'crimes' were as simple as being Catholic or Jew or homosexual or political dissident all found themselves numbered, stripped, hosed down, beaten, and degraded in countless other ways, all because they didn't fit into a particular mold. As we silently entered the parade ground, we were all struck by the lingering presence of evil and by an overwhelming sense of the magnitude of loss and tragedy. In the same buildings where inmate after inmate faced hostile stares and immeasurable humiliation, we viewed large scale pictures and a documentary with real people in real suffering. In the two barracks that were still standing, we were profoundly disturbed by the limits of a human being's personal space and comfort. How could anyone forced to live like this make it through alive, let alone with any sanity? As we wandered (and wondered), we came to the crematorium, that building where the guards burned the bodies of those who had died by disease, malnourishment, or violence or hanged from the rafters and then burned those unfortunate enough to be alive before entering the crematorium.

As I stumbled outside of the building, momentarily cut off from our group, I was paralyzed by the sheer enormity of evil and suffering in that place. I asked God the age-old questions, "Why did this have to happen?" and "How can one be a person of hope in a place like this?" I walked a few feet farther and saw to my surprise, a small square of grass and, in the middle, a tiny white flower. I realized that this was one of those moments when I was actually aware of God's continued presence and spoke a prayer of thanks. I then became aware of the probability that this small white flower of hope was made possible, not only because of God's love, but also because of the ashes of those who had died there. My prayer and placing of a stone on a marble table near the sign NEVER FORGET was that I would always remember three things: those who had died, that evil does exist and rears its ugly head all too often, and that God brings hope to a troubled world. Incidentally, a young woman who attended World Youth Day and this Dachau experience, was visibly shaken and deeply upset, not only on reflection of this evil, but also reflecting on some of the pain and suffering of her own life. Having this experience of hope enabled me to listen better and reach out to her in her need.

While reading *Victor Frankl's Man's Search for Meaning*, I became conscious of the fact that he was a prisoner on the very grounds where we had visited. His search for meaning (discovering that he who has the <u>why</u> to live can bear with almost any <u>how</u>) through shock and hopelessness, emotional death and finally the acceptance of his freedom, happened at least partly in that evil place. It is a testament to Frankl that he experienced the atrocities of this and other camps, and, very clearly, founded logotherapy, a field of psychology which is all about an attitude of hope:

> "and focuses on the future, that is to say, on the assignments and meanings to be fulfilled by the patient in his future." (3)

His positive perspective on life and on suffering held hope and promise, not only for his own spiritual being, but for fellow camp inmates and for future patients. For those who lost this faith in the future, death was imminent. Frankl observed that, with a person's loss of belief in any future, he also lost his spiritual hold (4) Frankl later calls this loss of feeling that life has any meaning an existential vacuum (5), a concept which really sucks!

While Frankl did not specifically declare what this 'spiritual hold' was or where this search for meaning originates, it is implied that a Supra-Meaning (Supreme Being?) gives rise to these ultimately spiritual yearnings. In fact, according to Frankl, it is a personal God who resides in the heart and soul of human beings, a God who enables the longings of all people to seek fulfillment and peace. When Frankl asserts that there are three ways to find meaning in life, he calls for a deeper awareness and need to be inspired by core values, values which are associated with the human spirit. Experiential values are those where true love is experienced, where art or music are truly appreciated, where encountering another person is (what I believe) respecting God's presence in them. Creative values are those gifts which we have been given, when used well, bring beauty and satisfaction. Attitudinal values include those traits of courage, compassion, determination, humor (and even suffering) which prompt us and others to look at the world differently. There is meaningfulness even in suffering, for, without suffering and death, human life cannot be complete. The Christian faith would affirm this by saying that, without the death of Jesus, there would be no resurrection.

Thomas Groome tells a story about Birute, a young woman who survived horrible atrocities in Lithuania when the Soviets invaded her country. The woman believed that God suffers when humans suffer. This faith carried her through unspeakable acts of abuse and degradation. She was able to display that attitude of hope, finding meaning and purpose in her suffering. Groome writes:

> I asked Birute how she and the Lithuanian people endured it all. Without hesitating she said, 'Our faith saved us.' I probed, 'But did you not feel abandoned by God?' She said, 'Never! Instead we came to understand what the cross really means for Christian faith-not that God sends suffering but that God suffers alongside us when it comes.' (6)

The bitter-sweet seasons of Lent and Easter give a spiritual thumbs up to Birute and Frankl's desire to find some meaning, whether in a camp or on a cross.

Finally, Frankl's theory that each person is responsible to find his or her own meaning in life and has choices to make those discoveries is an exhortation to all of us. He states that:

> ...man does have a choice of action. There were many examples, often of a heroic nature, which proved that apathy could be overcome, irritability suppressed. Man can preserve a vestige of spiritual freedom, of independence of mind, even in such terrible conditions of psychic and physical stress. Everything can be taken

from a man but one thing: the last of the human free-
doms-to choose one's attitude in any given set of circumstances, to choose one's own way. (7)

Believe it or not, Hollywood proclaims this mantra in many
movies of heroes who touch our hearts and our conscience. Stories
about people who rise above the suffering and pain of their lives tend
to capture our attention, our People's Choice votes, and our imagina-
tions. Attitudes of hope in the midst of hopelessness open our minds to
a resurrection-type message of suffering.

The main character in the movie *Life Is Beautiful*, (8), for
example, uses humor and optimism as a means to help his son and
other prisoners find peace in their own trials. The meaning of his life is
displayed in his sacrifice of self, in his desire to see his wife (like Frankl)
and protect his child, and in his joyful suffering. Both the Life Is
Beautiful character and Frankl were able to not only find meaning in
desperate situations but help others within their suffering. They looked
at their tragedy differently, and, in turn, found solace and spiritual strength
for themselves and others.

Also, the main character (Mel Gibson) in the movie, *Signs*, (9)
overcomes his own grief and hopes in the midst of hopelessness (in
this case, an alien mystery). Graham Hess, in a monologue response
to his brother's angst concerning uncertainty and fear, says that two
kinds of people exist, those who believe and hope and those who don't:

> People break down into two groups when the experi-
> ence something lucky. Group number one sees it as
> more than luck, more than coincidence. They see it as
> a sign, evidence, that there is someone up there,
> watching out for them. Group number two sees it as
> just pure luck. Just a happy turn of chance. I'm sure
> the people in Group number two are looking at those
> fourteen lights in a very suspicious way. For them, the
> situation isn't fifty-fifty. Could be bad, could be good.
> But deep down, they feel that whatever happens,
> they're on their own. And that fills them with fear.
> Yeah, there are those people. But there's a whole lot
> of people in the Group number one. When they see
> those fourteen lights, they're looking at a miracle. And
> deep down, they feel that whatever's going to happen,
> there will be someone there to help them. And that
> fills them with hope. See what you have to ask your-

self is what kind of person are you? Are you the kind that sees signs, sees miracles? Or do you believe that people just get lucky? Or, look at the question this way: Is it possible that there are no coincidences?

In each movie plot and in Frankl's real life story, those who have an attitude of hope and faith are able to not only make the best of the situation, but also grow and become stronger because of it!

Awareness: The Bigger Than Me Picture

On a September morning in 2001, Frank Silecchia laced up his boots, pulled on his hat, and headed out the door of his New Jersey house. As a construction worker, he made a living making things. But as a volunteer at the World Trade Center wreckage, he just tried to make sense of it all. He hoped to find a live body. He did not. He found forty-seven dead ones. Amid the carnage, however he stumbled upon a symbol-a twenty-foot-tall steel-beam cross. The collapse of Tower One on Building Six created a crude chamber in the clutter. In the chamber, through the dusty sunrise, Frank spotted the cross. No winch had hoisted it; no cement secured it. The iron beams stood independently of human help. Standing alone, but not alone. Other crosses rested randomly at the base of the large one. Different sizes, different angles, but all crosses. Several days later engineers realized the beams of the large cross came from two different buildings. When one crashed into another, the two girders bonded into one, forged by the fire. A symbol in the shards. A cross found in the crisis. "Where is God in all this?" we asked. The discovery dared us to hope, "Right in the middle of it all." (10)

A coincidence or a God-incidence? It is all in awareness. How come some see this symbol as the presence of God, while others only see steel and iron? Why was it that some immediately despaired and lost hope, while others who experience tremendous loss found fortitude in faith?

One who experienced tremendous loss during 911 and was able to see the bigger picture through it all was Lisa Beamer. Her husband, Todd, was killed in the crash of a plane controlled by terrorists and heading to Washington, DC for unknown havoc and disasters. Leaving a pregnant wife and two little boys for a typical day of business meetings across the country, Todd would spend the last minutes of his life praying over the phone with a customer service manager, then storming the cockpit with other passengers. After finding out about the tragedy that took her husband's life (and the lives of the 39 other passengers and crew on United Flight 93) and through the shock and grieving, Lisa's response was one of faith. In *Let's Roll*, Lisa writes about two particular Scripture verses that gave her hope and helped to calm her broken heart. One passage served to give healing and peace after her father's death when she was 15, then again helped in dealing with Todd's death:

> Oh, the depth of the riches of the wisdom and knowledge
> of God! How unsearchable his judgments, and his paths
> beyond tracing out! Who has known the mind of the Lord?
> Or who has been his counselor? Who has ever given to
> God, that God should repay him? For from him and through
> him and to him are all things. To him be glory forever!
> Amen (Romans 11:33-36)

Lisa comments:

> "Following September 11, I saw firsthand many dear
> people who were trying their best to cope with loss, hurt,
> anger, fear, and a host of other feelings. Some had lost a
> husband, father, daughter, mother, or friend. They wanted
> to soar like eagles; they deeply desired to get on with life.
> They wanted to look on the bright side and do the things
> the clichés recommend, but they didn't have the strength.
> Worse yet, they had no hope. My family and I mourned
> the loss of Todd deeply that day…and we still do. But
> because we hope in the Lord, we know beyond a doubt
> that one day we will see Todd again. I hurt for the people
> who don't have that same hope, and I pray that some-
> how the events of September 11 will encourage them to

investigate the possibility that faith in Jesus really is the answer to all of their life questions." (11)

   While Lisa's strong faith gave her hope in her loss and despair, 911 forced us all to see our lives as subject to the whims of those who hate, to the winds of violence that many use as instruments to a perceived goal. Pope John Paul II spoke often of a certain 'culture of death' that wraps itself around our relationships, institutions, political structures, media messages, and ways of dealing with each other. 911 proves that we are far from achieving a 'culture of light and life.' What does that tragic day in 2001 do to those people who try to live by faith and justice? Can our awareness be stretched to see that God was always and will always remain an active part of our suffering and dying?

   If we were to consciously gaze on the faces of faith like Beamer and Silecchia and see how they were aware of the greater picture (and a great God!), we might find an answer. It is the same awareness that Martin Luther King had as he was battling discrimination, discouragement, and depression, especially in the last days before his tragic murder. In his own suffering, he realized that God's grace picked him up. He confesses:

> Having to live under the threat of death every day, sometimes I feel discouraged. Having to take so much abuse and criticism, sometimes from my own people, sometimes I feel discouraged. Having to go to be so often frustrated with the chilly winds of adversity about to stagger me, sometimes I feel discouraged and feel my work's in vain...But then the holy spirit revives my soul again...And each of you in some way is building some kind of temple. The struggle is always there. It gets discouraging sometimes. It gets very disenchanting sometimes. Some of us are trying to build a temple of peace. We speak out against war, we protest, but it seems that your head is going against a concrete wall. It seems to mean nothing. And so often as you set out to build a temple of peace you are left bewildered. Well, that is the story of life. And the thing that makes me happy is that I can hear a voice crying through the vista of time, saying: "It may not come today or it may not come tomorrow, but it is well that it is within thine heart. It's well that you are trying." (12)

Maybe Fr. Joe Breighner, national speaker and newspaper columnist best sums up that Holy Spirit revival when he uses the symbol of putting a fork in a coffin. Relatives would tell him when he was growing up to 'keep your fork for dessert.' He always knew, as he grasped his fork, that something better was coming. An awareness of God's loving presence in the world, even in incredibly 'hopeless cases' like 911 or a concentration camp or an invasion in Lithuania or a persecuted prophet of civil rights, means that we know something better is coming.

For Mark Hart in Blessed Are The Bored In Spirit, and for many others, that 'something better' is God's unending grace.

> For example, He's bigger than suffering. When our lives are full of pain, when everything is blood, sweat, and tears, whenever we feel abandoned and left to suffer, we have to turn to God. Not partially, not halfway, but completely and totally...When we give God control, he reaches out to us just as Jesus reached out to Simon Peter as he began to sink after his steps on the sea. His Holy Spirit is just one prayer, one movement of our heart away. Christianity is not about immediate gratification; it is about immediate grace. Christ is a Savior, not a Santa; a God of faithful fulfillment, not an ATM of 'quick change.' (13)

"Something better" is the awareness that a loving God, a Savior, a Strength beyond all struggle is right there with us in our suffering. It is the awareness that there must be a greater power in control because humans like us tend to screw it up quite a bit! It is this belief that gets people like Liz through suffering. Although she lists two different scenarios of the pain of loved ones, she can also see God's healing power in each one:

> My Grandmother ("Mongy") dying- I doubted why he took her at that time. I questioned what kind of God would take her from me. I questioned that I was ready to handle her death. I was depressed and I wondered if faith mattered to me anymore. Then I realized... that my Grandmother was now with God and my grandfather. I knew that she never wanted to lose her independence and she died before she did. So I realized that what I thought was so awful for me might have in fact been what my Grandmother would

have wanted. I'm not going to lie, it hurt, it still hurts but I can understand.

Last year I realized that my friend was anorexic. I was really worried about her, but she continued to push me away. I started to doubt why God thought I could handle it. I was very depressed, hurt and emotional about the situation. Another friend said to me "If God brings you to it He will get you through it." And He did, He surrounded me with other great friends and although my friend is still sick, I have learned to cope with it better on my own. {Liz from Maryland}

Not all have the perspective that Liz has come to know. Many people get caught up with the unfairness of life, somehow shocked and disappointed that life is not living up to its part of the bargain, that things should really be better than they are...After all, didn't Jesus promise somewhere that our lives would be easier with Him? In reality, NO! But, He will give us strength and healing...

As I write this book, a brother and sister, both in high school, have just today lost their father, four months after losing their mother. I cannot imagine the grief, pain, confusion, frustration and anger they must feel and can only hope that they experience the love of God through their aunt who has taken them in and through people in our church and community. Unfortunately, there are no shortcuts through the suffering that life sends our way, no ways to detour the unfairness that sometimes makes us angry and afraid. There are no detours around evil, natural occurrences, being in the wrong place at the wrong time, having 'terminal life.' (We all will die someday!)

It would have been easy for Jesus as God to bypass the whole Garden of Gethsemane thing and go straight to the Resurrection, to say that it really was the Father's will that the cup pass from him and move on. And yet, Jesus went from the accolades of Palm Sunday to the agony of the garden, from the Calvary cross to the grave, and only then to the empty tomb! Martin Luther King, in his persecution and pain, recognizes the cross of Jesus as a reality (and a hope) in his own life:

> The cross we bear precedes the crown we wear. To be a Christian one must take up his cross, with all of its difficulties and agonizing and tension-packed content and carry it until that very cross leaves its marks upon us and redeems us to that more excellent way which comes only through suffering. (14)

This awareness is the long and short of all who suffer; it is what makes us disciples of Jesus. The death of Jesus on a cross is just another example of violence unless we experience the stone rolled away from the tomb. And, the Resurrection can only be seen in light of the suffering and death of Jesus.

Action: Looking for God in all the right places

As I drove around the day after the devastating tsunami a few years back, I asked God why this had to happen, why so many lives had to be lost in the name of 'natural disaster' (sometimes called an 'act of God' by insurance companies!). JUST THEN A VOICE SPOKE TO ME…Okay, it was really a very clear insight which I will consider God speaking to me in my questioning. "Faith is believing even when there are reasons not to believe." I can't prove to you or make you believe that God spoke these words of hope and clarity to me but I do believe they were not my words… heck, they weren't even where my mind, heart or soul were at the time. In that time of questioning, I found God was right there speaking to me. In fact, on further reflection, I realized I may have been asking the wrong question! Maybe, for humanity, the question should not be 'Why did this happen?' but "How does God want me to act in this evil or suffering?"

I remembered a beat up statue at a retreat house where we stayed one weekend. We called it the 'missing hands' statue. Gone were the outstretched hands (and arms!) of Jesus and only stumps remained. A young person took up a collection to fix the statue, but the monk who took care of the grounds refused it. He told us that many had offered donations to repair the hands, but that it served as a reminder to all that 'we are Jesus' hands in the world, that we are asked to reach out when others are hurt or in pain.' In a famous prayer attributed to St. Teresa of Avila's, she echoes the monk's message. She prays:

> Christ has no body on earth but yours, no hands but yours, no feet but yours. Yours are the eyes through which Christ's compassion for the world is to look out; yours are the feet with which He is to go about doing good; and yours are the hands with which He is to bless us now.

Fr. Joe Breighner too, in <u>When Life Doesn't Make Sense,</u> suggests our role as the hands and heart of Jesus when he states: "We humans seem so reluctant to get the message that we are created 'in the image and likeness of God.' When we reach out to each other in love, we reveal the face of God!...We become the way God gets into the world. The problem with so much of the mystery of suffering is that we struggle with the mystery of life. We keep looking for God somewhere else. The people who missed God the first time around in human history were looking for God somewhere else. They didn't expect to see God in swaddling clothes as a baby in a manger. They didn't expect to see God as a carpenter. They didn't expect to see God as an itinerant preacher. They didn't expect a God who would suffer and die...We are no different from them. We keep looking for God to work some miracle coming out of a cloud, and we forget that God wants to work a greater miracle of love by coming out of us!"(15)

This 'miracle of life' symbolism was made very real when Helene, a friend of mine who served as dean of a local college, was speaking to a Muslim student leader at the college. The young woman's brother had just gone crazy and shot innocent people at a movie theatre. She was angry at her brother but especially mad at God, wondering why Allah didn't stop her brother from inflicting such harm on innocent people. Helene became aware that the same God with whom she was angry was the same God who allowed my friend to be present to her in her anger. Although the young woman was not at a place where she could easily see God's loving presence, Helene was open to being used as an instrument of healing and peace. Where was God? God was right there with them as my friend and the young woman spoke. God was there to comfort and give peace to those who were hurt by her brother. Such is the miracle of love!

Dr. Anne Kaiser Stearns in Triumphant Survivors, suggests there are three responses of people who have had significant loss or suffering. Some never fully get over it and their grief permeates their life; some heal only to the point they were before their loss; and then there are those who not only recover but are actually better persons for it! One specific 'triumphant survivor' was the founder of MADD (Mothers Against Drunk Driving} who, because of her own loss, was able to change laws, raise awareness and challenge people's perspectives.

...This Spirit that motivated her to create something to save the lives of others is, I believe, the work of grace, the work of God within her. The grace, the presence of

God, is available to all, but due to our inner brokenness, not all of us will respond to God's presence. Even the presence of God within us will not take away our free will. (16)

Triumphant survivors, like this woman and like so may others throughout history (Frankl, Beamer, King, Silecchia, Birute, Jesus! and more) are those who take action and make a difference, even in their loss and suffering. These brave examples call us all to attitudes of hope amidst hopelessness, awareness of the bigger picture especially God's presence in the suffering, and actions on behalf of God to those who mourn.

In conclusion, attitude, awareness and action are three lessons we can learn from people who have had considerable suffering. It is only then that a death or illness or natural disaster or violence has any meaning, and only then will our faith grow in hope and love.

Questions for Reflection:

1. What suffering (your own or others) has brought about questioning?

2. What might you say or do for someone who has experienced suffering?

V. SPEEDING & SIN

I have a confession to make. When I first got my license, I soon broke some laws. 6 months after that alleluia day at MVA where I got my license, I was on my way to college and I failed to fully stop at a stop sign. An officer pulled me over and gave me a ticket, to which I replied, "Oh, sorry about that! Thanks and have a nice day!" The next time was 6 months later...I was going, well, fast on the interstate and was flagged down by a trooper. She said that I was 15 miles over the speed limit, to which I replied, "I was just keeping up with the traffic." The next time was a year later... You see, I had been to traffic court twice and had all but court costs taken away. I was speeding once again, and, as the police lights flashed in my rearview mirror, I thought to myself, "Don't these people have anything better to do, like apprehending serial killers or something? I mean, everyone else is speeding, too! It's not like it's a real crime or anything!" After grudgingly receiving yet another ticket and mumbling less than kind words under my breath, I faced another trial date, this time getting a higher fine....Fast forward about 10 years....

I was working as a church youth minister at the time and was at a meeting about 30 minutes from the church. The principal of the parish high school called the meeting and said, "Pat, you need to get back to the school. A student, Denise (name changed), is suicidal and she is asking for you. I got in my car, intent on getting back to the church. As I drove along, slightly speeding this time, (have you guessed yet?) a police officer followed me and motioned me to pull over. When I identified myself and explained what was happening back at the school, her response was, 'Tell it to the judge!" I went to court, armed with a letter from my pastor and from the principal, outlining what had occurred that day. The judge, after taking the letters and hearing my story, looked at my previous driving record, gave me a hefty fine and a point on my license. I realized then that my record had caught up with me.

Some of you may be calling me a speed junky or a sinful person.

Others may be wondering why I got such a bad rap from the judge the last time. But your question might be "why would I make this confession to you in a book on doubting?" I'll tell you now…I believe that the times we fail to love God, ourselves or others (my simple definition of sin!) are sometimes the cause of our doubting God's existence and personal presence in our lives. When we feel far away from God it is because we move away through sin.

I have an extreme challenge for you. Do me and yourself a favor… Read the above 'speeding' story again and put in any sin that you have (or have heard about). There are habits that we have gotten used to which make it very easy to rationalize. The story points to a danger pertaining to the use of your conscience. When I broke the law at the stop sign, I was apologetic and repentant. By the third time, however, I was blaming the police officer for picking on me! You see, feeling guilty should never be the litmus test for whether an action is right or wrong. We can always deceive ourselves and rationalize our actions by what others are doing worse or by saying that we are not really responsible or by some other habitual form of excusing ourselves

Look at the word RATIONAL LIES. Like me, you may tend to make excuses or lies that sound very rational to you but, after careful conscience-checking, are not really the way you intended to act or even feel is the right way to act. Most of us have a set of criteria that we have learned about what is right and what is wrong, about how we should live lives and how we should not, about what we should think or do and what we would never think or do. Lifestyle issues like sexual activity or using people, drug or alcohol abuse, lying or cheating in relationships or at school, gossiping or rumor-milling, profanity or impatience when dealing with people, viewing pornography or other destructive materials, buying too much or too much concern over money are only some of the areas that we tend to rational lies.

Interesting too is a certain Hebrew word meaning repent. Metanoia, or repentance, is a 'turning away from sin and turning back to God.' Any time we rationalize our wrongs, we turn away from God. It is sobering to see the number of young people (no, people in general) who have spoken to me about feeling far away from God, when in reality, it is people who have done the turning away! Many believe that God is always loving, always present, always inviting us to know Jesus more deeply. And yet, some are surprised when, after sinning, they cannot find God. Is it possible that God is still there but we need to turn away from sin and around 360 degrees (figuratively and practically) to see God? Many people claim that they 'wander' in sin or 'lose direction' for a time. It fits, doesn't it, that our turning away sometimes confuses the way and we don't know (or care) how to get back to God.

How do we lose our way and wander through sin? Why do we turn away from God and do (or not do) things that keep us facing in the wrong direction? Although there are many different rationales or reasons that people give for their actions, I have chosen three phrases to describe this time of wandering away from God: selfish search, selective ethics and shaking of the soul. Maybe this can be a starting point in our honest appraisal of what we do or don't do that can draw us away from experiencing the presence of God.

THE SELFISH SEARCH:

I was hiking through a pretty dense part of the woods. I don't remember why I was looking down; maybe it was to watch my step, but probably because I was mulling over some problem in my mind and not being cautious. Anyway, I looked up just in time to get a hanging twig in my eye! It hit at the perfect time and place so that, while I didn't get a painful scratch on the eye itself, I did have a nice cut below my eye for a couple of weeks! I don't think I really did anything wrong in this instance; in fact, not watching where I was going was the only thing for which I was guilty!

And yet, we can be guilty of what I call 'naval gazing.' When we get so caught up in looking down and inward that we forget about everyone and everything else and only focus on ourselves, we might be blameworthy. Dorothy Day, Catholic Worker movement originator and advocate for justice and peace, writes about an 'adventure in prayer' that she had while traveling on public transportation. Instead of looking down on this bus as many do (and have you ever been in an elevator?), Day watched a homeless man and had a revelation of sorts:

> And now I pick up Thomas Merton's last book, 'Contemplative Prayer...' and the foreword by our good Quaker friend Douglass Steere brought back to memory a strange incident in my life. He quotes William Blake: "We are put on earth for a little space that we may learn to bear the beams of love."
>
> And he goes on to say that to escape these beams, to protect ourselves from these beams, even devout

men hasten to devise protective clothing…Suddenly, I remembered coming home from a meeting in Brooklyn many years ago, sitting in an uncomfortable bus set facing a few poor people. One of them, a downcast, ragged man, suddenly epitomized for me the desolation, the hopelessness of the destitute, and I began to weep. I had been struck by one of those 'beams of love,' wounded by it in a most particular way. It was my own condition that I was weeping about-my own hardness of heart, my own sinfulness…I think that ever since I have prayed sincerely those scriptural verses, "Take away my heart of stone and give me a heart of flesh."…so that I may learn how to truly love my brother because in him, in his meanest guise, I am encountering Christ. (1)

When all of our actions are self-motivated/self-centered, when we have a heart of stone and when we are constantly looking for ways to build ourselves up or get ahead (no matter the cost to others), we are guilty of naval gazing or having an expanded ego! EGOtistic people have the tendency to Edge God Out of their lives. They may turn away (or inward) and miss the presence of God around them, even missing answers to questions of faith and neglecting the needs of others.

Miguel, a young man from Georgetown University who Colleen Carroll interviews in her book, The New Faithful, observes how he selfishly acted in college:

We used to like talk the talk but not walk the walk. I really abused the gifts God has given me, all to the glory of Miguel. There wasn't anything compelling me, absolutely no introspection. I just acted. And the culture allows you to act like this…I'd been trying to fill myself with self-love. I was trying to find God in women and in relationships. I realized then that what I had been looking for was God. (2)

Miguel's honest admission about edging God out of his life and replacing God with his own selfish desires was the first step in a closer walk with God. His egotistical naval gazing, if you will, was not reflecting at all on his actions but doing whatever made him feel satisfied at the time. By his own confessed self-love, he edged God out. There was no room for God! It is this lack of introspection, this looking out for selfish gain, which causes many young people to doubt how God is working in their lives. In fact, many times, doubts about the world around us and God's loving presence in that world can be caused by focusing only on ourselves and missing God's greater picture. "Well, I really wanted to get that job, God. Why didn't you help me?" "I prayed to you for this relationship to work. It's your fault that it didn't." Or trickier still. "Why did you have to take my friend/parent away from me?" Case in point...

Mary (name changed to protect the innocent) was a young woman I had hoped to date at some time in the future. In high school, she was going with Jim but I just knew that she didn't have the best man. That was me, and I would treat her like she deserved to be treated, with love and respect, with flowers and candy! In college, I asked Mary out and she said yes! I was floating on a cloud for seven months, so happy and in love until...Mary said that it might be a good idea to 'go slower' or even stop dating for awhile, since she was transferring to another college. I begged and pleaded, not only with Mary but with God. "Mary, I can understand your need to go to school, but I think our relationship is important enough that we continue it" (secretly praying that she not go away and that we marry someday!) To God, I remember saying, "Why does it have to be this difficult? I know that you have brought us together. Why can't we just get married!" What happened next? You guessed it...Mary and I broke up.

Angrily and tearfully, my prayers were about questioning God, asking why God didn't answer my needs in this relationship...Recently, as I watched my wife and three kids at our dinner table, I prayed in thanks for 'unanswered prayer.' I thanked God for not listening to me in the way my limited thoughts and feelings wanted God to listen. For, if Mary and I had made it through that time and had even gotten married, there are no guarantees that my life would be better than it is now. I have a very loving wife and great kids and I can't imagine a better life!

Certainly, our limited vision and our EGO get in the way of what God has in store for us. Certainly, the sins of Adam and Eve come back to haunt us anytime we think we have all of the answers and can, without consequence, eat of the wrong tree and play God in any given situation. One need only watch Bruce Almighty (3) to be reminded of the perils that befall people who try to play God (Remember the post-it notes in Bruce's rooms? Or the 'problems' with weather decisions? Or the mess that he makes with just one relationship?) The selfish search can make us more lost than we need to be…we can simply turn back around to God.

SELECTIVE ETHICS:

Bono, lead singer for U2 but also activist, humanitarian and prophet, when asked to comment in an interview about good and evil in the world, speaks candidly and personally,

> Look: evil encroaches in tiny footsteps on every great idea. And evil can almost outrun most great ideas, but finally, in the end, there is light in the world. I accept that God chooses to work with some pretty poor material. But I'm much more amazed by what people are capable of than I am by what they're not capable of, which is to say that evil doesn't surprise me…I do see the good in people, but I also see the bad-I see it in myself. I know what I'm capable of, good and bad. It's very important that we make that clear. Just because I often find a way around the darkness doesn't mean that I don't know it's there. (4)

As Bono suggests, there is a tension within all of us when deciding between good and evil or making any moral decisions. It is a tension or a tendency to choose the selfish solutions (see last section) over that which might benefit others. It is a tendency to succumb to the pressures and temptations of this world, or, more dangerously, to choose the easy way, the shortcut, the I-am-not-responsible way. Because we have the ability to freely choose, we also have the ability to make big mistakes in our choosing! One of the mistakes we make is to think that 'freedom is all about me' and the choices are all mine to make.

Chris and Linda Padgett, in their book entitled <u>Not Ready for Marriage, Not Ready for Sex,</u> write candidly about dealing with temptations to be sexually active in their high school dating relationship, but received two different messages about their sexual freedom. Chris' mom taught and lived a moral life based on biblical standards. Chris' divorced father, however, thought differently:

> When I was growing up, my father made it clear that if I treated a woman with respect by considering her sexual happiness and not merely my own, then I should not be ashamed to practice safe sex…Many times I

embraced the freedom my father's approval gave me. Nevertheless, I couldn't silence the warning voice of God within when I crossed the lines in physical intimacy...When I numbed myself to the truth, my spirit was never fully at peace. (5)

I'm sure you have heard similar definitions of freedom. Freedom is doing anything you want to do, as long as it doesn't hurt anyone else. And yet, this line (of hurting anyone else) has some cracks. First, can you always know if you are hurting another person, say with engaging in sexual activity or with addictions? Second, how about the ways we hurt ourselves by not living the way we should? The temptation to freely choose evil is an insistent one, some might even say from the devil! Maybe Mother Teresa said it best in A Simple Path when she was writing about God's test for us:

We are all capable of good and evil. We are not born bad: everybody has something good inside. Some hide it, some neglect it, but it is there. God created us to love and to be loved, so it is our test from God to choose one path or the other. Any negligence in loving can lead someone to say Yes to evil, and when that happens we have no idea how far it can spread. That's the sad part. If someone choose evil, then an obstacle is set up between that person and God, and the burdened person cannot see God clearly at all. That's why we have to avoid any kind of temptation that will destroy us. We gain the strength to overcome this from prayer, because if we are close to God we spread joy and love to everybody around us...Christ's love is always stronger than the evil in the world, so we need to love and to be loved; it's as simple as that. (6)

Mother Teresa speaks a universal truth about good and evil. The more we choose to do evil, the harder it is to see God's goodness in our lives. Although some have hit the 'rock bottom' of evil and can rebound to turn their lives around, many make a habit of choosing evil and cannot see a way out. According to Mother Teresa, prayer gives us the strength to turn back around and make better choices.

The word 'selective' in selective ethics brings to mind that choice which we have because of God's free will gift. Free will is a gift and a responsibility. It is a gift because we are able to decide to do right or good, or to do wrong or evil. There is a healthy balance between our personal responsibility and asking God to be the center of our lives. While God does not require us to follow some pre-destined plan for our lives, God does want us to choose what is right and good. It must pain God to know that we have this choice and abuse it on a regular basis! Father Joe Breighner clearly articulates about the gift of free will:

> God, in creating us, loved us so much that he gave us the absolute power to choose, even to choose against him, even to choose to reject him! Given the terrible devastation that humanity has wrought through our use of free will, there are those who ask why God would have given us free will, knowing in advance, as God, some of the terrible ways we would use it? I surrender that question to the mystery of love. If you love someone, you have to give them freedom. (7)

Father Joe here makes an analogy concerning addictions. In AA and other addiction help-groups, a key to break the addiction is to make day to day choices about being sober, including the recognition that there is a higher power to help us. Another key to sobriety is to help someone else in their addiction, which, in turn, helps the helper!

> The irony is that we find our freedom only by surrendering to God...In short, when we use our freedom to love the way God loves us, we become our best self and become truly free. (8)

Freedom, then, is the ability to select ethics or make choices that will make us the best we can be, the people that we are called by God to be. We can only know true freedom by giving ourselves over to that higher power and by helping other people. Whew, is that real freedom? Yes, if we think beyond 'free will' and personal decisions as tools that are all-for-me and of a selfish nature, and start viewing our gift of freedom as a partnership between human beings and the God who created us.

SHAKING OF THE SOUL

It struck me recently how many things require shaking in our world. Whether it's a bottle of juice, a canister of whipped cream or a can of paint, one of the most popular directions on household items is to 'shake well before using.' That got me thinking about a verse I read in Hebrews: 'His voice then shook the earth; but now he has promised, 'Yet once more I will shake not only the earth but also the heaven.' This phrase, "Yet once more" indicates the removal of what is shaken as of what has been made in order that what cannot be shaken may remain. When bad things happen, and God knows they do, I often get nervous thinking that my faith will be shaken. That need not be the case. In reality, tough times can be God's way of shaking me free from false gods and worldly ways that I'm hanging on to. He's rattling me for my own good, so that I'll be left with the unshakeable-God, the beginning and end of my life. What things in your life, what false gods is our Lord trying to shake out of you? (9)

Is it possible, as Mark Hart reflects, that God could rattle our souls, if you will, for the purpose of waking someone up from a 'sin sleep?' Some of us wake up pretty easily in the morning, others must be prodded and cajoled out of bed. Maybe God allows us to experience questioning or doubts (a shaking if you will) so that we take a more honest look at our lives and what we need to change. Here we go again...The 'turning away from sin' that we discussed earlier doesn't always come naturally. We have to be shaken from the slumber of habits that are deeply ingrained, aroused from the lethargy of addiction, stirred up to go out and be better people. Remember my speeding story? It took me three tickets and years of driving to be shaken from my 'need for speed.' More importantly, I was able to learn about the 'ripple effect' of bad choices when I received the ticket for a fairly noble reason! My bad record from the past had caught up with me, reminding me to drive more carefully and not make any more excuses! This was a shaking I needed!

And how about Saint Peter, loving and simple apostle of Jesus, first Pope of the Catholic Church? Even THE ROCK was shaken in an earthquake kind of way. After Jesus patiently taught him and the other apostles his message and Messiahship, then asked Peter to stay awake while he went to pray in the Garden, Peter feel asleep! Then, if that wasn't enough, Peter also denied even knowing Jesus, not once, not twice but three times (John 18)! As you might expect, Jesus' beatings, crucifixion and death really shook Peter and the other apostles. But, Jesus appears after the Resurrection and asks Peter "Do you truly love me?" three times and commands Peter to "Feed my sheep." (John 21) It is only after Jesus shakes Peter with those three questions that he was able to rebound and return to lead the early church.

One more thing about shaking…Sometimes we are totally off-base, heading the wrong way on a road of sin and don't even know it! I like to hike. I obviously like to get lost when I hike, because I do it so well! One day, after a pretty long hike through many miles (and two parks!), I started back to my car. Running out of time, I passed a landmark that I knew well and thought I could turn right and take a shortcut through the woods. Adding three miles onto the hike was not my intention…but that is what I got in place of my shortcut! I felt helpless and frustrated, which made finally finding the car even more exhilarating! I thought I knew the way and even had confidence in my ability, yet I was mistaken.

Have you ever had that experience in your life? Have you ever thought that you were on the right road but a different point of view (sometimes but not always a friend or family member) called you back on track? Have you ever been sure that you were acting in a righteous and holy way, only to discover that your motives were less than admiration and you were, instead, judging others?

One of my favorite movies is Saved, (10) which, through the use of exaggerated stereotypes, asks the viewer some pretty pointed questions about who is saved and who isn't. Is it the person claims to love Jesus and those actions don't follow their words OR is it the 'sinful ones' engaged in premarital sex (including homosexuality), smoking, drinking and other forms of 'unholy living' but who treat everyone else with respect and dignity? Of course, the black and white depictions of these characters are suspect, but I do think one particular dialogue as worthy of consideration. After Hilary Faye (popular young Christian) attempts an exorcism of Mary (pregnant teen who slept with boyfriend who is homosexual to change his mind), the following dialogue ensues:

Hilary Faye: Mary, turn away from Satan. Jesus, he loves you.
Mary: You don't know the first thing about love.
Hilary Faye: [throws a Bible at Mary] I am FILLED with Christ's love! You are just jealous of my success in the Lord.
Mary: [Mary holds up the Bible] This is not a weapon! You idiot.

How does someone get so far away from the truth as to throw the very Book which speaks of unconditional love, mercy and forgiveness? Better yet, how does someone get such a limited vision of who God is and what a personal relationship with Jesus is all about? It is called sin and someone is in need of some shaking! But, aren't we all guilty when we judge others before looking at ourselves or when we fail to take responsibility and attempt to rationalize our action away by blaming them on others. Mister Rogers (of 'the Neighborhood' and cardigan sweater fame) got some shaking one day at church. He writes:

> ...I heard the worst sermon I could have ever imagined. I sat in the pew thinking, "He's going against every rule they're teaching us about preaching. What a waste of time!" That's what I thought until the very end of the sermon when I happened to see the person beside me with tears in her eyes whispering, "He said exactly what I needed to hear." It was then that I knew something very important had happened in that service. The woman beside me had come in need. Somehow the words of that poorly crafted sermon had been translated into a message that spoke to her heart. On the other hand, I had come in judgment and I heard nothing but the faults...Thanks to that preacher and listener-in-need, I now know that the space between a person doing his or her best to deliver a message of good news and the needy listener is holy ground. Recognizing that seems to have allowed me to forgive myself for being an accuser that day. (11)

Finally, because of sin, we can feel far away from God, in fact, blaming God for the distance we've caused! Our selfishness gets in the way of seeing God's unselfish love and healing. Our selective ethics keeps us from embracing the gift of 'true free will' in our lives. And, our sinful habits and disease of judging others before ourselves makes us ready for a little shaking.

As we 'speed' through life, let us remember to put the blame (and the credit) where it is due. It might be a really good idea to take an honest assessment where some of our doubts originate. Is God away from us or might we be possibly moving away from God?

Questions for Reflection:

1. What is your 'speeding story,' a time that you rationalize a sin?

2. How does sin keep you away from seeing God?

VI. DIRECTIONS
FOR THE DARK:

My wife and I had gone away to a bed and breakfast in West Virginia for our anniversary. On our way to dinner one night, we both remarked about the incredibly starry and clear sky. We stopped outside, breathing in the crisp air and staring into the night. I caught movement out of the corner of my eye and realized I had just witnessed a shooting star. " Look, Lee Ann, a shooting star!" I exclaimed. But, she had missed it. In fact, she rather disappointedly told me that she had never seen a shooting star and would have to take it on faith that there even existed such a thing! Since she has a rather extensive scientific background, I found this statement very interesting. As we continued to stand there, trying to pinpoint the direction of other shooting stars, I asked if it was faith in me or what she had learned and come to believe concerning the sciences. She simply said, "It's both, Pat. I believe that I must trust you and others whom I love (especially God) for what I have not yet seen myself. Yet, I also trust in science and medicine and systems of proof that I have studied because God has also revealed creation through that." At that point, we witnessed the longest shooting star directly in front of us, careening from east to west across the sky!

Taking it on faith? Trusting science, medicine, systems of proof and God? In a sense, the discussion that resulted from the shooting star experience seems simplistic and even insulting to those who are asking questions about spirituality. I hope that I have not tried to give simple answers to complex faith questions, yet have provided some material to better explain what might be happening in your search. And yet, this chapter takes things a bit farther in that it offers practical suggestions on what to do when you doubt. While I am not recommending that any of us take it on 'blind faith,' there are concrete steps that can be taken to help you find your shooting star, or at least know what direction to look.

Long-time youth worker and teacher Mike Carotta offers a '3-D view of spirituality' (directions) for young people. Since we began this book with the image of doubting as 'crawling in the dark,' it is appropriate to speak in terms of providing direction and taking steps to make it through. What Carotta suggests and what I will expand on is a solid outline of down-to-earth strategies for finding your way through any time of searching or doubting.

> The three directions are vertical (relationship with God), horizontal (relationships with other people) and internal (emotional)…The task…is to pay attention or try to glimpse the dominant direction of spirituality (and to) nurture the other less-developed directions…(1)

I will be adapting these important directions a bit, and propose the following meanings for each direction: **Vertical direction** is indeed our relationship with God and/or spirituality in general. Like all of our relationships, a vertical direction takes time and energy, and I suggest prayer and meditation as opportunities for healthy vertical growth. **Horizontal direction** is the way we interact with the world around us, from our connections to a faith community and spiritual guide(s) to finding 'safe places and people' to ask the deeper questions. **Internal direction** deals not only with emotional growth, but also intellectual stimulation and the ability to make moral choices based on our belief systems. Each of these spiritual directions is a lifelong process of discovery and growth which fits with the image of spirituality as natural as our need for water. Let's get started, then…

Vertical direction is our relationship with God and/or the spiritual world. It is how we work through the deeper questions in life (purpose, suffering, etc) and who (if anyone) we look to in time of need or struggle, joy or praise. It is our image of God and how we intensify or grow in that relationship. One of the most awesome descriptions of vertical direction was given in a talk by a priest friend of mine. Speaking to a group of young leaders from churches and schools, he said, "Prayer is expressing your soul to God, letting your spirit breathe!" As humans, we have the natural inclination to breathe the spirit, to express our souls.

Matt, a young man I had worked with previously, called me out of the blue to talk (and I think to express his soul!). He is living in Colorado and is newly married. Matt now works as the head graphic artist of a medium sized corporation. Although I had not seen Matt for a long time, I remembered him as an extremely funny young man in high school, always cracking jokes (sometimes at my expense) and giving one-liners that would have everyone falling off their chairs. He was and still is an extremely gifted artist, and his style was cartoon characters (sometimes me) and comic book heroes. He had been and still remains a deeply sensitive and spiritual person, someone who cares for others and gives generously from the heart.

He and his wife were expecting a baby and he wanted to not only tell me, but 'pass some things by me.' Matt no longer considered himself a Catholic. He was a self-proclaimed deep thinker and good person but did not hold to the belief that the Catholic Church had the Truth or that God existed in the image Catholics projected. I told Matt that I believed it was God all these years who gave him the gift of creativity, expression, compassion and thinking deeply. I suggested that, if he looked back on his life in high school and college, he might see how God had impacted it, even when he was questioning things. It was quiet on the phone for a moment, and then Matt said, "You know, Pat, I expected you to say some faith thing like that!"

Was my conversation with Matt on a spiritual level? Of course. Was he thinking deeply about life's meaning? Absolutely. Is Matt working in a vertical direction? I believe he is, although he may not even know it. While Matt may not be currently connected to any faith community besides his family (see importance of this in horizontal direction section), he is probing the spiritual world, sifting through profound issues of the soul. And yet, my challenge to Matt still stands and can serve as a possible direction for all who doubt. Let your own soul breathe!!!

Take some time to reflect. Think about your past year, or simply think about your past week. Are there any people who might have shown you the image of God? Was there a particular place (a sunset, the beach, the woods, a river) which might have helped you to experience the peaceful presence of God? Better yet, take 5 minutes tomorrow morning and ask God to help you to be aware of the presence of Jesus in your life? When I was in college, I was going through a painful doubting time. I asked Fr. John, a trusted friend, what to do. I will always remember his advice, "For the next three weeks, pray each morning for hope. Just say, 'Jesus, please give me hope today.' And then, look for it!" Not understanding the simplicity of the directions, I asked for clarification. He said, "Just do it!" Over the next three weeks, I prayed every morning for hope...and you know what? I found it because I was looking differently! So, ask God for hope or a better understanding of Jesus' presence in your life...5 minutes...every day. And, if you want to get really gutsy, take 5 minutes at night to list the ways you saw Jesus' presence and that hope. I am not kidding. You may be amazed how He is already there! Andrea exhibits a real trust in her own vertical prayer and Jesus' active presence in her life:

There are always people in my life which I could turn to for help, such as my friends and my youth minister, but they are not first on my list, God is. God is the great counselor, and he has knowledge that far surpasses that of humans. Therefore, I take up my case with God, and if he tells me to seek human guidance, then I will do so. Yet God alone is perfect, and he alone knows my innermost thoughts, he alone knows who I am, and therefore, God, and not I, should have the first say in what I should do when I doubt. He is the first that should offer me council and support, and it is to Him that I turn first. {Andrea, Minnesota}

Andrea is speaking from a vertical direction, expressing the importance of her relationship with God. Sometimes our prayer, like Andrea's, gives us peace and calms our restless spirit. Bono of U2 describes a calm that prayer and meditating bring in the midst of his chaotic life:

I will say this: there's a noise that you see on the surface, a kind of certain frenetic hyperactive person doing lots of things, with lots of interests and ideas that I'm chasing. But below that, really, at the very bottom of that, there is…peace. I feel, when I'm on my own, a peace that's hard to describe, a peace that passes all understanding…Reading, praying, meditating. It might be just walking around. People often say to me: "How do you do all that stuff? You're doing this, you're doing that." I guess that's probably how…you can call it a Sabbath moment, if you want, because the Sabbath day was a day of rest. (2)

Sometimes, though, our vertical relationship with God is hard to experience because of the loudness of life. Sometimes, our prayers are less than attentive and our surroundings less than quiet. Fr. Ronald Rohlheiser quotes the very human holy man, Henri Nouwen, as Nouwen describes prayer for himself:

My time apart is not a time…of deep prayer, nor a time in which I experience a special closeness to God; it is not a period of serious attentiveness to the divine mysteries. I wish it were! On the contrary, it is full of distractions, inner restlessness, sleepiness, confusion and boredom. It seldom, if ever, pleases my senses.

But the simple fact of being for one hour in the presence of the Lord and of showing him all that I feel, think, sense, and experience, without trying to hide anything, must please him. Somehow, somewhere, I know that he loves me, even though I do not feel that love as I can feel a human embrace, even though I do not hear a voice as I hear human words of consolation, even though I do not see a smile, as I can see in a human face. Still, God speaks to me, looks at me, and embraces me there, where I am still unable to notice it. (3)

Henri Nouwen saw the importance of praying, even if he did not always feel like it or see the merit of it. As I learned with my 5 minute prayer for hope, taking time to pause and ask God for an awareness of Jesus' presence is enough (even pleasing) for God.

And talk about Jesus' presence...Sometimes I think Catholics have the best kept secret around (why it is kept a secret is the topic for another whole book!). I am not speaking about the Gnostic Gospel of Thomas or where the treasures of the Vatican are buried! I am alluding to the "source and summit of our faith!" (4)

The Sacrament of the Eucharist is not having a symbol of Jesus in us; it's receiving the real thing! Mark Hart reveals the secret of this incredible sacrament:

How many millions of people hit their pillows every night wishing, hoping, praying for true love, selfless love, life-giving love? How many hours, days, and months are spent in regret because of love lost? And yet, perfect love exists in the Blessed Sacrament in virtually every city, country and language. The opportunity to love and be loved is present globally. The world cannot quench our hunger but this Eucharistic daily bread can. The words of the self-help gurus cannot lift our spirits or souls the way that the Incarnate Word can. No game of golf or walk in the park will fulfill our need for rest as the Sabbath day does. (5)

Receiving the Eucharist, I mean, really receiving the power and presence of Jesus' Body and Blood means that Jesus wants to physically and spiritually be in us, coursing through our bloodstreams, an intimate part of our lives! This is sometimes a stumbling issue for people. How can this happen? Where is the evidence that this is even occurring! Why should I believe that I am receiving the real Body and Blood of Jesus? Certainly, it still looks and tastes like bread and wine...But the senses limit us in so many ways. Faith was never meant to be proven only through our senses, was it? There is something more happening here. I suggest that you do two things:

1. Take some time to sit...alone...in front of the tabernacle (where the Eucharist is kept).
2. Take a look at the people around you.

Take some time to sit alone...One of the greatest complaints about the Mass that I hear from young Catholics is that it is boring, repetitive and not relevant to them. Many of you (and many adults) are waiting for an earth-shattering spiritual experience to suddenly happen: Maybe the altar will open, catch on fire and God will speak from the center of it! Maybe the priest or minister will start speaking in a different language that only you can understand! Maybe you will hear something that will totally and radically change your life and finally make you happy! I am not saying that God won't ever choose one of these ways to come to you, but, why wait around? Worship is not really for our benefit, but for God's glory! The more we become engaged in worship and prayer, the more happens! When we, as the Body of Christ, involve ourselves (mind, body, spirit) in prayer and worship, even singing (God forbid...oh, no God doesn't!), great things transpire! If you feel so inclined, say a prayer of hope or ask that God help you to see more clearly what the Eucharist is all about.

Take a look around you if you are in church. Look at the persons next to you, those who wear faith on their faces and those who wouldn't know a smile of joy if it bit them on the...well, anyway, look around. You are seeing yet another miracle. You are seeing the Eucharist right there in the flesh! In fact, say a prayer during the service for the baby crying, the single parent, the elderly man, all sitting near you. Instead of looking at each person in the communion line and placing judgment on clothing, hair style or other looks (we all do it!), pray for each of them.

When the priest breaks the host, we are not only celebrating Jesus' awesome presence for us, not only remembering Jesus' broken body and sacrificial death on the cross, but we are remembering that we as the Body of Christ are sometimes pretty broken too. The person sitting next to you may be the answer to your questions or, chances are, you may be the Good News to them! The Eucharist is not just something to cling to; it is something real to be shared with others. Pretty incredible, huh?

A word about Scripture…I am not one to randomly open the Bible and start reading the first passage where my finger rests, although I have heard that others do this. In my zeal during high school, I did try to read the Bible from cover to cover…not a good idea…I never seemed to make it through Leviticus! And yet, there is something to be said for bringing the Word of God off the shelves and begin reading! I suggest the Psalms since David is very candidly and simply writing about his spirituality, with its joy and sorrows, struggles and praises! Or read the Gospels, meditating on the parables and even making yourself one of the characters in the story! "Who in the story do you relate to the most? Why?" "What were you thinking or feeling when Jesus said…" Or, better still, take a specific suggestion from one of my heroes, ex-President Jimmy Carter when he advises Isaiah 63: 15 and 17:

> The honesty and passion of Isaiah's prayer impress me. It's a cry of anguish, of suffocation, or abandonment, of disappointment. He didn't do what many of us do, which is simply complain about our problems. He approached God directly. Nor did he pray in a superficial, rote manner we often adopt-reciting a few traditional words for perhaps sixty seconds a day. He leveled with God in an intensely personal way (6)

Don't discount locating a bible study for people your age. There are many age groups which meet to plow through the richness found in the Bible. In fact, spiritual groupings such as a bible study help in our horizontal directionings and can serve as another safe place to ask questions!

Horizontal directions are the ways we interact with the world around us, specifically how we give and receive love and how fruitful we are in sharing our spirituality. Do you have a connection to a faith community? Is there a safe place you can go to not only listen, but to ask the tough questions of life? Do you interact with creation in ways that are life giving and sustaining or in ways that destroy life?

One of the mistakes people make concerning spirituality is focusing on the vertical relationship between God and me. It is a mistake because it is unbalanced. Going to a church service and 'praying your heart out' is very uplifting and good…unless you judge another's appearance throughout the service or give the finger to someone for cutting you off in the church parking lot. And, if you listen well to Scripture but do not pick up Jesus' messages of justice, peace, servant leadership and unselfish love for your own life, you are missing half the Gospel!

Henri Nouwen, a priest and prophet of the poor, in a letter to young people in Baltimore, expressed this relationship with others as a requirement for all humans. Because of our connectedness with one another, we are responsible for one another. We are asked to be fruitful in our lives, even through the doubts and other times when our faith feels weak. Nouwen writes:

> Fruitfulness is what Jesus calls us to. Not successfulness. Successes come from strength and power. Fruits are born in weakness. Jesus was born in weakness and died in weakness. His life was a failure. But very very fruitful. You fruitfulness starts in community. When you come together as a fellowship of the weak, always willing to forgive and be forgiven, then you start experiencing the fruits of the Spirit among you: peace, joy, gentleness, perseverance and most of all love. These are the fruits that the world is waiting for. These fruits will not be brought by individual heroes or great stars who know what everybody should do, but by small communities of faith who are like lights in the midst of darkness... (7)

Horizontal direction means faithfully reaching beyond yourself to make a difference in this broken world. Whether on the streets with people who are homeless or in our own faith community, horizontal direction points us all away from ourselves and to others. Robert discovered this for himself in a justice program sponsored by the Catholic Church:

> Justice Walking, a challenging nine month program based on Jesus' call to build the kingdom of God through justice and peace, ironically further shook my faith. In the end, though, the doubt I incurred through J-Walking seems to have been divine providence. It helped me realize what Jesus really meant when he called us to be Christians—and it wasn't what I was used to. I

had always championed Catholic social teaching and did reach out to others, such as at Catholic Charities, but J-Walking truly brought about the beginning of a conversion. Each month we met at a soup kitchen to eat with the homeless. We eliminated misconceptions and rightfully restored ourselves to the same level with them. As I was exposed to the brokenness of our world, I realized how broken I am, too—how torn and entangled, confused and frustrated, insecure and alienated, alienating and judgmental, and co-responsible for the violence and suffering across the world—and yet also how interconnected and interdependent with all humans I am. More so than before, I could now enthusiastically embrace the salvation Jesus offers. Doubt brought me closer to Jesus. He didn't just share his food with the poor—he invited them into his home to eat with them as friends! {Robert, Kentucky}

Although Robert realized more fully his responsibility in the church and understood more clearly some essential Catholic teachings, there is a growing trend to claim a personal spirituality while also divorcing oneself from any institutional religion. (see Matt's comments above) Well-intentioned young people (and adults) say goodbye to Sunday services and any other church connections, but pray, read and meditate on their own. And I have seen countless young people approach doubts in this way, choosing to go it alone and totally cut themselves off from that which they are questioning. I don't recommend this, not just because I am a Catholic youth minister! No, for many reasons, this can be the unhealthiest thing to do. David Tacey, a widely respected psychologist from Australia, recently wrote The Spirituality Revolution. In a speech introducing the book's themes, Tacey insists that God is not dead and neither is religion. He also proposes that faith communities need spiritual searchers and spiritual searchers need a home.

We are all spiritual beings. Those who are involved in religion have made an important choice about our spirituality...The spirit must not be confined to the internal world, although it can begin there. The Spirit with us is a universal Spirit and needs to be shared. It can be personal but never private...Spirit is inherently communal and inherently wants to be shared with others and realized in the presence of others. (8)

Thomas Groome also shares this sentiment. In a chapter entitled, *What Is Our Heart's Desire-Growing Spiritually For Life*, Groome says:

> Spirituality without deep roots in a religious tradition may not weather the storms of life. Trying to go it alone spiritually, without a faith community, seems foolhardy, even a bit of a contradiction. Life-giving spirituality is surely relational; remember, we are 'made for each other.' On the other hand, religion that does not nurture people's spirituality is as dead as a doornail. (9)

Yes, connecting to a faith community is not just your responsibility but your right! Many of us have encountered a faith community that is, shall we say, less than welcoming of young people! Are you seen and not heard at your church or are you embraced as important members of the Body of Christ? Are you welcomed as full and active participants, even serving as leaders and ministers, or do you feel pushed to the side? Dr. Robert McCarty, executive director of the National Federation for Catholic Youth Ministry, affirms the role of young people and places a challenge before you and all faith communities:

> Every young person should be connected to the life of the faith community. Instead of looking at young people as the church of the future, look at them as the young church of today. The faith community is energized by the presence of young people in liturgies and on committees…(10)

Again, young people and others who seek answers to faith questions need a community of believers, a safe haven if you will, just as religion needs to be open to asking those questions. In presenting results from the College Transition Project, authors Kara Powell and Krista Kubiak state:

> Perhaps the most significant finding of the CTP to date is that students who felt like they had a safe place to talk about doubt showed greater faith maturity. Whether it was with the youth group overall or with a specific adult leader, students who had the opportunity to struggle with tough questions and pain during

high school seemed to have a healthier transition to college life…Perhaps it's the depth that comes from the well-processed tough times that builds roots that can withstand the shifting winds of college life. (11)

According to this article, a person's transition from high school to college, usually a very difficult physical and spiritual adjustment, can be made a bit easier with a 'safe place.' Whether it be in a specific youth grouping or generally in a larger faith tradition, a community based on beliefs and structure can provide stability in uncertain and changing times. 22 year old Andrea from Oregon comments that her faith provides an identity when she is still discovering who she is. There is certainty and freedom in knowing that, while many things are changing, her religious identity and community remain the same. Andrea says:

When I was a freshman in college, the search ultimately brought me to an encounter with God, and my life has never been the same since…after the experience, I became much more serious and purposeful in my faith. I discovered that the narrative of God's love for God's people reveals a very different kind of freedom: the freedom to never again have to worry about whether I am somebody, because the living creator of the universe says that I am. The freedom to know what story I'm a part of and to whom I ultimately owe allegiance. (12)

Locating a spiritual mentor and meeting with that person on a regular basis is a good way to expand your horizons (and your horizontal direction!) I suggest a wise adult with whom you feel comfortable, someone who is youth-friendly, accepts you, listens well but will also challenge you spiritually. Jane says:

Having other adults around with whom to talk is the best way to deal with doubting. My youth minister Molly is such a strong person and when I am wondering if God exists she reminds me all the reasons I believe that he does. The other adults that help with youth group also help me deal with the tough faith times. The Mass is another way that I deal with my doubt and questions of faith. If there is no God, then why each week all around the world do people cel-

ebrate him. I don't think it is just for the heck of it!
There is something about the fact that we are all connected through the Eucharist that helps me remember
that God is bigger than me and yet he cares about me
so much! {Jane, Minnesota}

Caitlin from DC was also able to share with a spiritual guide
when she was going through doubts concerning confirmation and teachings of the Catholic Church. After some prodding from parents, she
decided to talk it through with the parish youth ministry coordinator:

My parents suggested that I meet with the Coordinator of Youth Ministry at our church, but for a while I
pushed the idea aside. I wanted to handle things my
own way. For the time being, I continued to follow
their plan, but knew the whole time in the back of my
mind that I was not changing my mind... But on a
retreat, something happened; something clicked and
changed inside of me. I heard stories from other young
people in our church of how they had found God in
their own lives, and I knew that I could easily find
ways to see God in my own life. I grew more confident in my faith and I found that I actually wanted to
try going through the confirmation process. Halfway
through retreat, we received letters from our parents.
My mother wrote a letter to me that changed the way
I felt about Catholicism and myself. I do not remember exact words from her letter, but I do know that it
inspired me. I went up to the youth coordinator, and
asked him if we could meet and discuss my thoughts
on the faith. He was more than happy to meet with
me and honestly talk to me. He helped me realize that
I was allowed to have some doubts in Catholicism,
and that it was healthy. I became conscious of the
fact that I really did enjoy Catholicism and that I wanted
to continue in that faith for the rest of my life.

One of my favorite Scripture passages is the Emmaus story,
tucked away at the end of the Gospel of Luke (24: 13-35). Two disciples of Jesus were deep in conversation, painfully grieving and dis-
cussing his recent death by crucifixion. A stranger appears and begins
asking questions. They are astonished that the stranger seems to have

no clue about the headliner of the day. "What do you mean, you don't know that Jesus died? He was supposed to rise again, but..." The stranger (Jesus) listened and was present to them, much like a spiritual mentor, not only on the road to Emmaus but later at an inn during the breaking of the bread. Find someone like this, willing to share in your journey through questions, joy, doubt and dinner!

Internal Direction deals not only with emotional growth, but with intellectual stimulation and the ability to make moral choices based on our belief system. It means, in a sense, that we are open to taking a second look at how we feel, think and act not only as we search through life's fundamental issues, but at all times. On faithsite.com, the reflection for Matthew 14: 22-36 (Peter and walking on water) is this:

> Someone said, "The cure for love at first site is often a second look!" The theme of today's reading could easily be, "The cure for a doubting faith is often a second look."... The focus of the disciples on the powerful winds and tossing waves created fear and doubt in their hearts about their safety. Even when Jesus had identified himself and empowered Peter to walk on the water, the doubt of the disciples was greater than their faith. When Jesus saved a sinking Peter and still the storm, the disciples took a second look at Jesus... There will be storms and dark nights in your soul journey. If they create doubt in your heart, all we ask is that you give Jesus a second look. (13)

To work on internal direction, then, means to maybe take a step out of the fishing boat, to have a new vision, to look for a second time at whatever you have taken for granted.

For me, it is the Eucharist and other Traditions of the Catholic Church that I have known for awhile, but don't always experience personally, sensually (with the senses, of course!), intellectually and with the heart. How about you? Is there any second look that you need to take?

For world champion figure skater and Catholic Kimmie Meissner, taking a second look meant reflecting on her life and making a promise to grow inwardly. In an interview with The Catholic Review, Kimmie spoke of internal direction when she said:

> My New Year's resolution this year will be to stay

true to myself-with so many outside influences it is
not always as easy as it sounds; also to have faith in
the choices I make and to open my heart and mind to
the possibilities. (14)

For some people, taking this internal second look has meant
not only growing inwardly in a emotionally mature way, but also learning more about their faith with an 'intellectual rigor,' as evidenced by
24 year old David Legge of Yale Law School in The New Faithful:
...an intellectual interest in the Catholic faith of his
childhood that had surfaced during his second year at
Yale still lingered in his consciousness. Earlier that
school year, while reviewing a paper he was writing
about Abraham Lincoln, Legge had realized that he
had never applied as much intellectual rigor to the study
of his faith as he had to his schoolwork. "I thought,
you know, I know so much more about Abraham Lincoln than I do about Jesus. And Jesus should be so
much more important in my life. Maybe I should learn
something about him." (15)

Legge started by reading the Bible and Catechism of the Catholic Church, then graduated to the Catholic classics like St. Augustine
and Thomas Merton, eventually becoming a regular attendee at Mass
and other church functions. This newfound understanding of the need
for knowledge and the passion that accompanied it, caused Legge to
not only take a second look at the Catholic Church but also his own
lifestyle choices. As Legge and others like him take that second look
and realize the richness of scripture and traditions in the church, they
begin examining their lives, their conscience, and the other voices com-
peting for their spiritual attentions. After reflecting very closely and
carefully, many also make gradual changes in their values systems and
choices.
Although the idea that sin (or turning away from God) as a
cause of doubt was covered earlier, there is an effective way to decide
if you are internally heading in the right direction when making moral
decisions. I have designed a simple four-step process to use when you
are faced with a moral dilemma or temptation to do something that
may turn you away from God's loving and freeing will. DELAY-PRAY-
PLAY-REPLAY.
The first step, to DELAY, means to carefully and consciously

call to mind the various values foundations or belief systems that you have relied upon in the past. Of course, there are times when we are confronted rather spontaneously by temptation (such as what to do at a party) and have very little time to think, let alone delay. And yet, it is important to know what you believe and why you believe so you are ready to stand up for or against when the situation arises.

PRAY is the second step, and, although this seems pretty basic, it really means inviting God to be in control, to give you the strength to make the right decisions. To really pray means to surrender and say "I can't do it alone!" When my own son and daughters were younger and we were hiking or climbing, I would always tell them that they should never say "I can't." They had (and have) two powerful options: Try harder or be able to ask for help. Praying means that we ask God for help and direction, since trying harder in making moral decisions isn't always possible.

PLAY frees us to make the decision, hopefully that we know God will bless. There is also a responsibility to face the consequences for our decisions, especially if it is not a choice that God will bless! This is an important step for a couple of reasons: One, many people are paralyzed by indecisiveness and uncertainty and this enables those people to fulfill Nikes' PR message: Just Do It! Two, when we willing and freely play by making a certain decision, we are also taking personal responsibility for that decision. In a culture that thrives on blaming anyone and everyone, this empowers people to risk success and sometimes failure.

REPLAY means to evaluate our decisions and intentionally choose what actions we will repeat and what actions we will never try to do again! An incredible way to replay our decisions is to participate in the wonderful gift of the Sacrament of Reconciliation. Through an examination of conscience, we are able to think about those areas of sin where we failed to love ourselves, others and God and work to change the behavior and thoughts that led us to sin in the first place.

I love Indiana Jones (16) movies and one of my favorites is The Last Crusade. In the last 15-20 minutes of the movie, Indiana Jones must endure a series of tests to reach the Holy Grail, the cup that Jesus drank at the Last Supper. The first one has to do with kneeling before God; the second is professing the name of God, the third taking a leap of faith (it is interesting that Dr. Jones, the academic, must make a choice that has everything to do with faith and little to do with science!). But maybe the greatest test comes in the room with the Grail...and a very, very old knight... and an evil Nazi millionaire...To choose poorly means knowing about Jesus but dying a painful and gruesome death (I'll let you guess who dies!) To choose wisely means knowing the person of Jesus and inheriting eternal life. (I'll let you guess who receives this!) Anyway, the point is in the choosing.

If you are living a life of making risky or unhealthy choices and if this is turning you away from God or a life-giving spirituality, you have the mechanisms to make changes. Take a second look at the origins of your questions or apathy. As you may recall, there are some causes for doubting that are entirely natural and good, while others, like turning your back on the good and true, may need some rethinking!

Questions for Reflection:

1. Which is your strong direction (vertical, horizontal, internal)? Weak?

2. Who or what can help you provide direction for your faith?

VII. WELCOME HOME

Crawling in the dark...buckets of water...voices within and outside... attitudes, awareness, and action...speeding and sinning...3 directions... I have offered many different symbols as images of the searching spirit and what can specifically be done during doubting times. And yet, these symbols are only tools to explain and maybe motivate. The real light comes when you are honest and face your faith questions with openness, determination and courage.

But if from there you seek the Lord your God,
you will find him if you look for him with all your heart
and with all your soul...(Deuteronomy 4: 29)

The real light is the promise that God gives to those who search, to those who are open, to those who seek with all of their spirituality. The joy that we as kids felt when we found someone after an intense game of hide-and-seek is a small measure of the joy in the journey of discovering who God is and whose we are.

May God bless you as you crawl through the darkness towards the inevitable light of hope and love. May God bless you not only in your crawling, but also in your search with safe places, good companions and the peace and confidence that you need to be strong. May God bless you as you come to know what I have experienced, that our God is a loving and gracious God, wanting us to know Jesus in a deeper way, and giving us the Holy Spirit to live our lives with truth, reverence and courage.

In closing, I leave you with a song by popular youth conference performer, Steve Angrisano, who also wrote the forward to this book. Loosely based on the parable of the Prodigal Son, it is an invitation to anyone who has been away, to anyone who has been crawling around and looking for the light. It is an open-arms-no-holds-barred greeting from the God who gave you the thirst to question and wishes to quench that thirst with His loving presence; the same God who wants to be The Voice in your life; the same God who is there to hold us when we suffer; the very same God who has been standing next to us when we have turned away.

Welcome home!

WELCOME HOME,
By Steve Angrisano

Welcome home, welcome home;
so far away, so long and so alone.
The journey's not been easy,
the road, it seemed so long.
It matters not now, child.
Oh, welcome home.

Hollow dreams, like the desert sand,
can shine so bright but slip right through your hands.
The treasure you were seeking
turned out empty in the end,
but your heart knows what it's after,
so come on in.

Though you think this journey's over
feel you lost out in the end,
funny thing is, now it's over,
it finally can begin.

Far and wide,
your soul will seek to find a love that quenches your heart's need.
But none on earth can give you what so desperately you need.
There's only one true love that sets you free.

So the shattered heart you're holding
may seem fragile, may seem small,
but sometimes only when it's broken
will we let God have it all.

Matters not what you followed far.
It's love that brought you back here where you are.
See, nothing said or done will keep this father from a child.
Your heart could see the treasure all the while,
a heart that led you back here down this road that you know.
So fall into these arms child,
and welcome home. (1)

NOTES:

I. Crawling In The Dark

1. Cambridge Dictionary for American English, Cambridge University Press, 2007

2. Microsoft Encarta, 2007

3. Hoobastank, Crawling in the Dark, 2001

4. Lance Moore, 'Outdoors with God', Devotional Thoughts on the Great Outdoors, Barbour Publishing 2003, p. 154

5. John of the Cross Selected Writings, The Ascent of Mount Carmel, ed. K. Kavanaugh, Paulist Press, NY 1987, p. 85

6. Quote originally copied by hand at LeTenche, Mother Teresa Exhibit, World Youth Day, 2005 in Cologne, Germany. Hosted by Missionaries of Charity. Now published in Mother Teresa 'Come Be My Light': "The Private Writings of the Saint of Calcutta," ed. Brian Kolodiejchuk, M.C., Doubleday Press, New York, 2007, p. 164.

II. Natural Thirst

1. The Complete Works of Saint Teresa of Jesus, ed. E.A. Peers from the Critical Edition of P. Silverio de Santa Teresa, Sheed & Ward, London and New York 1946, p.78

2. Peggy Noonan, 'John Paul the Great,' Remembering a Spiritual Father, Penguin Group 2005, p.127

3. Dorothy Day Selected Writings, ed. R. Ellsberg, Orbis Books, NY 1983, 1992, p. 23

4. Ronald Rohlheiser, 'The Holy Longing,' The Search for a Christian Spirituality, Doubleday Press, NY 1999, p. 6-7

5. Thomas Groome, 'What Makes Us Catholic,' Eight Gifts for Life, Harper, San Francisco 2002, p. 7

6. Michael Carotta, 'Sometimes We Dance, Sometimes We Wrestle,' Embracing the Spiritual Growth of Adolescents, Harcourt Religion Publishers, Florida 2002, p. 20-21

7. Jimmy Carter, 'Living Faith,' Times Books/Random House, NY 1996, p. 16, 18, 22, 26

8. Alexandra Robbins & Abby Wilner, 'Quarterlife Crisis,' The Unique Challenges of Life in your Twenties, Penguin Putnam, NY 2001, p. 78

9. Kenda Creasy Dean, 'Practicing Passion,' Youth and the Quest for a Passionate Church, Wm. B. Eerdmans Publishing, Michigan 2004, p. 35

10. Reginald Blunt, 'In Search of Living Waters: The Seven Spiritual Yearnings of Youth,' in The Princeton Lectures on Youth, Church and Culture, Princeton Theological Seminary NJ 2005, p. 2-10.

11. Parker Palmer, 'A Hidden Wholeness,' The Journey Toward An Undivided Life, Jossey-Bass, CA 2004, p. 26

12. Thomas Groome, op. cit., p. 46.

13. Stacie Orrico, 2003, Virgin Records America, Inc

14. Kenda Creasy Dean, op. cit., p. 36

III. Strong Voices, Tough Choices

1. All Scripture References are taken from the New Revised Standard Version: Catholic Edition, Silver Burnett Ginn, 1993

2. Thomas Groome, op. cit., p. 82-83

3. The Autobiography of Martin Luther King, Jr., ed. C. Carson, Warner Books, Inc., NY 1998, p. 351

4. Michkas Assayas, 'Bono: In Conversation with Michkas Assayas,' Penguin Group, NY 2005, p. 125

5. Robbins and Wilner, op. cit., p. 56

6. Fred Rogers, 'The World According To Mister Rogers,' Important Things To Remember, Hyperion, NY 2003, p. 54.

7. Sean McDowell, 'True for You, but not True for Me,' Youthworker Journal, January-February, 2006, p. 29

8. Robbins & Wilner, op. cit., p. 10

9. Gene Monterastelli, 'How to Save the World and Retire,' Your Guide to Living a Life of Passion Without Going Broke, Brother Blue Publishing, DC 2004, p. 44-45

IV.   Suffering & White Flowers

1. Thomas Groome, op. cit., p. 90

2. Albert Camus, 'The Plague,' Vintage Books, NY 1948, p. 224

3. Viktor E. Frankl, 'Man's Search for Meaning,' An Introduction to Logotherapy, Pocket Book/Beacon Press, NY 1959, p. 152

4. Frankl, op. cit., p. 117

5. Frankl, op. cit., p. 168

6. Thomas Groome, op. cit., p. 172

7. Frankl, op. cit., p. 103-104

8. Life Is Beautiful, 1998, Miramax Films

9. Signs, 2002, Blinding EdgePictures

10. Max Lucado, 'Mocha with Max,' Friendly Thoughts & Simple Truths from the Writings of…, J. Countryman Press, TN 2005, p. 132

11. Lisa Beamer with Ken Abraham, 'Let's Roll,' Ordinary People, Extraordinary Courage, Tyndale House Publishers, IL 2002, p. 233

12. Autobiography, op. cit., p. 354, 357...This was on April 3, 1968, the day before he was assassinated.

13. Mark Hart, 'Blessed are the Bored in Spirit,' A Young Catholic's Search for Meaning, St. Anthony Messenger Press, OH 2006, p. 102

14. David J. Garrow, 'Bearing the Cross,' Martin Luther King, Jr., and the Southern Christian Leadership Conference, William Morrow and Company, Inc., NY 1986, inside cover page

15. Fr. Joseph Breighner, 'When Life Doesn't Make Sense,' Cathedral Foundation Press, MD 1997, p.147-148

16. Fr. Joseph Breighner, op. cit., p. 155-157

V.   Speeding & Sin

1. Dorothy Day, op. cit., p. 181

2. Colleen Carroll, 'The New Faithful,' Why Young Adults Are Embracing Christian Orthodoxy, Loyola Press, IL 2002, p. 136-137

3. Bruce Almighty, 2003, Universal Pictures

4. Michkas Assayas, op. cit., p. 85

5. Chris & Linda Padgett, 'Not Ready for Marriage, Not Ready for Sex,' One Couple's Return to Chastity, Servant Books, OH 2006, p. 58-59

6. Mother Teresa: A Simple Path, compiled by Lucinda Vardey, Ballantine Books, NY 1995, p. 51-52

7. Fr. Joseph Breighner, op. cit., p. 96-97

8. Fr. Joseph Breighner, op. cit., p. 102

9. Mark Hart, op. cit., p. 114

10. Saved, 2004, United Artists Films

11. Fred Roger, op. cit., p. 126-128

VI. Directions For The Dark

1. Michael Carotta, 'Nurturing the Spiritual Growth of Your Adolescent,' Harcourt Religion Publishers, FL 2002, p. 18-20

2. Michkas Assayas, op.cit., p. 318

3. Ron Rohlheiser, op. cit., p. 219

4. Catechism of the Catholic Church, United States Catholic Conference, 1994, #1324-1327

5. Mark Hart, op. cit., p. 44

6. Jimmy Carter, 'Sources of Strength,' Meditations on Scripture for a Living Faith, Times Books, NY 1997, p. 40-41

7. I wrote to Henri Nouwen on behalf of the Archdiocese of Baltimore Micah 6:8 Social Justice Weekend for young people and received both a call and a faxed letter from Nouwen on 2/5/93. Partial text included.

8. David Tacey, 'The Spirituality Revolution,' Psychology Press, UK 2004 Tacey summarizes key points in speech made in New Zealand.

9. Thomas Groome, op. cit., p. 273

10. Vincent Gragnini, 'Surviving in the West,' One Magazine, November, 2006, p. 18

11. Kara Powell & Krista Kubiak, 'When the Pomp & Circumstance Fades,' Youthworker Journal, September-October, 2005, p. 57

12. Robbins & Wilner, op. cit., p. 30

13. Taken from 2000faithsite.com Day 164-January 25

14. The Catholic Review, 'What Are Your New Year's Resolutions?' January 4, 2007.

15. Colleen Carroll, op. cit., p. 26

16. Indiana Jones and the Last Crusade, 1989, Lucasfilms

VII. Welcome Home

ABOUT THE AUTHOR

Dr. Patrick Sprankle (Pat), husband and father, is currently Director of Youth Ministry at St. Louis Church Clarksville, MD. Having served two parishes over a 25 plus year span, and has extensive experience with middle and high school young people and young adults. Pat graduated from Graduate Theological Foundation with a doctorate in Ministry (2007) and holds a Master's degree in Theology from St. Mary's Seminary and University (1995). Pat has written for Group Publishing, Priest Magazine, Disciples Now (Movie Reviews for a youth website), Silver Burdett Ginn (Connect with Music) and has an ongoing parent series with Cornerstone Media. Pat has also spoken and led retreats locally to over 50 churches and schools and has given presentations nationally in 7 states and youth conferences.